EMPOWERED SELF-CARE

HEALING BODY, MIND & SOUL FOR A BETTER WORLD

COMPILED BY AERIOL ASCHER
#1 INTERNATIONAL BEST SELLING AUTHOR

Empowered Self-Care
Healing Body, Mind & Soul For a Better World

Copyright © 2021 by Aeriol Ascher

RHG Media Productions
25495 Southwick Drive #103
Hayward, CA 94544.

The chapters provided by each of our co-authors are provided for information and education purposes only and are not intended to replace the advice of your doctor or health care provider on medical and/or health-related issues. Please consult your doctor or health care provider for advice on medical and/or health-related issues.

ISBN 978-1-7365189-0-8 (paperback)
ISBN 978-1-7365189-1-5 (hardcover)

Visit us on line at **www.YourPurposeDrivenPractice.com**
Printed in the United States of America.

ACKNOWLEDGEMENTS

I want to acknowledge the kindness, patience, and loving respect that our publisher Rebecca Hall Gruyter and her entire RHG media team displayed throughout the process of bringing this project forth. They went above and beyond to ensure that each chapter was an accurate representation of our hand-picked healers, teachers, and coaches and that their voices came through authentically to create this vibrant, healing collection.

I would like to thank my grandma, Lela Weiland, may she rest in peace. She planted a seed in me to always write my story down. I would also like to thank my mom, Carole Ascher, who I know loves me more than anything and whose generous sponsorship made this project possible.

I want to thank Caterina Rando, my esteemed sales coach and fun girlfriend. Her Thriving Women in Business community brings joy to my heart and empowers so many women to "expand their fempire!" Thank you for your brilliance, your friendship, and for always inspiring me to be loud and proud about the value I bring. Also, thank you for being one of the first co-authors to jump on board and believe in the **Empowered Self-Care: Healing Body, Mind, and Soul for a Better World** book project!

Of course, I would also like to express my gratitude to each of the co-authors who poured their hearts and loving essence into this project and lent their wise voices to these pages.

Thank you to all my healing clients who were willing to try virtual self-care to keep me going during the shelter-in-place crisis.

Thank you to our **BodyMindSoul.TV** & Media Network sponsors for your support in making all our programs possible.

Thank you to the listeners of our *Healing Body Mind and Soul* podcast for continuing to keep our voices alive and consciousness expanding by downloading globally.

And thank you to you, our dear reader. Thank you for opening your mind, opening your heart, and embodying your best self for a better world.

CONTENTS

FOREWORD

Dear Reader,

Thank you so much for leaning into this powerful book.

My name is Aeriol Ascher and it has been my great honor and pleasure to gather and connect this group of 25 holistic healing practitioners, spiritual teachers, and transformational coaches to synthesize and compile this book for you, our precious reader. It is our hope that this book will serve you in your own daily self-care practice, and serve humanity as a manual for soulful living and empowered self-care.

Our book's mission

The purpose of this book is to expand awareness, to raise the consciousness of humanity, and to heal our planet by empowering as many individuals as possible with the very best whole self-care wisdom, inspiration, and healing practices by experts, influencers, and leaders in the fields of holistic health and wellness, personal empowerment, transformation, and new thought leadership.

It is our belief that by co-creating this project as a collective (**BodyMindSoul.TV** & Media Network and our Associated Networks: RHG Publishing & Media Network and **VoiceAmerica.TV**) we can reach, impact, and empower the most people on the planet to heal themselves, and in doing so, heal the planet.

My personal mission

Why am I doing this? Honestly, I just cannot stop bringing my work forward! For several decades now, I have been on a divinely-driven healing mission to raise the consciousness of the planet. I believe that by educating and empowering people with self-healing wisdom, they can be more comfortable in their own bodies, more authentic and effective in their communications, and they can embody and bring forward a more powerful presence as a speaker or leader. Together we can start to create a better world for future generations to live in. This internal drive has led me to create an award-winning healing practice and an international network of virtual healers, psychic readers, and coaches available seven-days-a-week. I kept up a hectic pace for years, but let it go when I was led to pursue my own speaking career.

In 2019, about a year after closing my center and downsizing my healing studio to my home, I began compiling interviews of holistic health practitioners, spiritual teachers, and transformational coaches of all sorts on my "Healing Body Mind and Soul" podcast. Then in 2020, shortly after a global pandemic hit, I pivoted my healing practice and founded the **BodyMindSoul.TV** & Media Network. I created and produced the podcast and video series: *Self-Care Under Quarantine*, earning our network two communicator awards of distinction from the The Academy of Interactive & Visual Arts (AIVA).

Then I had this amazing vision: It came very clearly to me during a deep meditation during my bi-monthly float inside the isolation tank. In my mind's eye, I saw these lovely sparks of light— like little stars dancing around and swirling together into a vortex or geometries—landing into a magical-looking book. I swear, it looked like something out of a *Harry Potter* movie! With it, came a flood of energy and a subsequent outpouring of writing. I have to say, the vision inspired me so much, there was little else I could think of for months. It was the synergy of this project and the community of ladies that sustained me during the pandemic of 2020.

From this pivotal point, it became evident that the *Empowered Self-Care* book was the next natural step through which I could serve the greater healing-community as a whole. I think that publishing is the most powerful thing that a leader or speaker can do to position themselves as an expert. I also really enjoy being a video-creator and producing multi-media in order to raise the consciousness of the planet and usher in the divine feminine healing energy. I also enjoy providing the space, visibility, and exposure to my fellow practitioners, forward thinkers, and messengers to amplify their voices and messages in the world, so that they can uplift, inspire and empower humanity, and raise the consciousness of the planet.

By bringing this project forward, I feel I am not only creating a vehicle that is a powerful force of healing for you, the reader, but also showcasing the brightest and most caring souls that I have gathered together from across the globe. Together, we've created a worldwide network of support and healing that we can all tap into by combing through the pages of this anthology.

How to use this book in your own daily self-care practice

Of course, not every story will resonate with every person, which is why having this beautiful collection of chapters is so exciting. When I sat down to organize this book, I began weaving the chapters together in what I thought would be three sections: body, mind, and soul. But as I caressed the chapters forward, I noticed them taking on a life of their own. I let them tell me what they wanted, and soon the three sections began to reveal themselves:

- **Part One - Into the Deep: Loving the Self Whole.** In the first section, we will expand our definition of self-care and dive deeply into the body's innate wisdom and self-awareness in order to eliminate anxiety and pain. We will learn to communicate with the body as these masterful practitioners share their work.

- **Part Two - Focused Intention: Moving Toward Mastery.** In this section, we examine mindset, beliefs, and how both conscious and unconscious thoughts about ourselves shape our experience and our reality.

- **Part Three - Informed Guidance: Trusting the Self.** This section is about tapping into and trusting our inner-guidance to create our environment and inform a balanced lifestyle.

As you work your way through the book, here are three pieces of advice for embracing your personal empowered self-care practice and enjoying fully embodied, fully expressed, soulful living:

1. Take this book slowly. Let yourself reflect upon the stories and deeply process each chapter's energies. Try to absorb each chapter and follow up with the free gifts and offerings of each co-author. Journal either in our companion book, *The Empowered Self-Care Journal*, or a journal of your choice. Write down your reflections on each chapter, each story, and each exercise. Which ones resonate with you?

2. To further enrich your daily self-care practice, you may want to incorporate the Empowered Self-Care Wisdom Cards for divine inspiration, motivation, or daily reflection. Pick a card daily and write it in your journal as you focus your intentions for the day. Before you go to bed, jot down some reflections from your day and watch the magic emerge in your life! Shop for oracle decks and self-care support tools here: **https://aeriolascher.com/shop**

3. Get Support that suits you. Find yourself a coach or mentor who works for you and who can help you fully embrace your power to reach your self-care goals. Each of our co-author's has generously offered free exercises, free downloads, and other resources for you. I highly recommend you take advantage of their invitations to connect with you.

To further support the reader, I regularly offer "Five Week Virtual Book Club" discussion groups online. I would love to have you get involved in our self-care conversation at one of these live virtual book club events. You can view and sign up for upcoming offerings here: **https://body-mindsoul.tv/registration**

So, without further ado, I invite you to step into your own personal journey. The journey into your own daily self-care practice. It is my hope that you will shift and expand your definition of what self-care means to you, and that you will awaken an awareness of your own divinity that drives you forward in your life with passion and purpose.

To your success!

Aeriol Ascher
Holistic Educator, Intuitive Healing Master, Spiritual Guide
www.AeriolAscher.com
Empowerment Leader, Show Host, Book Compiler
www.HealingBodyMindandSoul.com
Creator, Founder, Executive Producer
www.BodyMindSoul.TV & Media Network

PART ONE: INTO THE DEEP

LOVING THE SELF WHOLE

HOME: A REFLECTION OF SELF
BY LINDA LENORE

Plants were drooping. Some leaves were yellow while others were brown, totally dried up. What had been a lush greenhouse window full of houseplants just a few weeks before was now a dismal array of neglected plants desperately needing some TLC (Tender Loving Care), just like their owner.

Decades ago I discovered houseplants portray a correlation between **how I was caring for myself**—a direct reflection of my lack of TLC to myself, a lack of SELF-CARE. Too little water (dehydrated), too much food (over weight), brown and dried up usually meant burnout had occurred, not enough sunshine (brittle bones, hair, and nails) or too little focus on a balanced and integrated body-mind-spirit connection needed for a healthy life!

Putting Others First

There were always reasons associated with my lack of awareness for what both my plants and I needed. Sometimes it was raising a family where kids came first, or the time my mom's health was failing from a rare disease and I was her advocate. Another time happened when my son had brain surgery, ultimately died, and my marriage ended in a bitter divorce.

The timeframe for this series of events lasted several years and took a great toll on all aspects of my health–physical, mental, emotional, and spiritual. With the loss of my deep spirituality, and then being diagnosed with cancer, I was at the lowest point in my life. I thought the only way out was suicide. I could go on, but you get the picture.

Along Comes Feng Shui

I was introduced to Feng Shui in the mid-1980's while attending an interior design conference. At that time no one knew what Feng Shui was, at least no one within my sphere of influence. This philosophy, religion, or whatever it was, smacked of voodoo, cults, anti-God, and almost every belief system of which I'd been warned of to be wary.

Then the speaker at this conference showed a picture of a home and its rooms. He made a statement so startling it cut me to the bone. As he pointed to one room in the picture, he said "A room like this, placed in a home like this, could cause health issues, even a child's death."

Those words echo in my mind, heart, and soul to this day. A Feng Shui mMaster said them as he described a home—MY HOME! My son, Jeff, having died a few months prior, had lived in the labeled room. It was a strange configuration I'd never seen before, and, thank God, haven't seen since.

Pray That the Journey Be Long

There are defining moments in our lives that change the trajectory of life in ways we've never imagined; this was a monumental one. It took me down an unknown path, a path about energy, home, health, and spirituality—a journey of breaking barriers, climbing mountains, crossing oceans, opening my eyes, and blowing my mind.

Words change lives: emotions shift our perception of reality. Time plays tricks on our body, mind, and spirit. During the next several years, I was guided along the road less traveled, a road not of my making. Divine intervention is the only logical explanation since I certainly didn't plan any of it.

My focus was to disprove this ancient Asian art of Feng Shui. Could it have predicted my son's death? Could it have prevented it? After months of searching, I finally found a class at the University of San Francisco, just the first of many, a 90-minute drive from where I lived. (Remember, this was pre-internet and Google and before any book was written on this oral tradition in the Western world.)

Years passed, workshops were taken, Masters sought. I gleaned what I could, but still, clarity was not achieved. The old quotation, **"when the student is ready the teacher will appear" happened to me.** I was attending a Feng Shui class and in the first 20 minutes this gentleman described a bedroom/bathroom configuration I had observed. There were women who were my clients living in the environment he described, who were experiencing serious health issues. Chills ran up and down my spine as he spoke. GOD-bumps appeared on the back of my neck and all over my arms.

Originally trained as a Traditional Chinese Medicine (TCM) professional, his focus was to KEEP patients healthy. If patients were sick, he treated them FOR FREE in his clinic until their vitality returned, at which point he sent them home.

However, he found that invariably a number of his patients returned with the same recurring health issues. This discovery at age 24, sent him on a new journey studying how the built environment affects humans. Could their homes be the cause of their illnesses? He found the answers within Feng Shui principles.

During that workshop I heard how the home affects every part of our life, especially our health. I discovered our home influences our future in myriad ways. The repetition of patterned energies within our home—the things we see and the things we do automatically, day-in-and-day-out, every day without thinking—create neuro-pathways in our brain, and these pathways become habits. The habits unconsciously affect our health, how we see ourselves, how we perceive our life, and how we interact with the world.

There, in a three-hour lecture, were the answers to many of my questions. Excitedly I arrived home telling my husband I had to learn from this master. The only challenge–this was the last seminar he would teach in the United States.

One week later I was in Canada, the month after that I was in Switzerland. Following months found me in various towns and cities in Austria, Germany, and Switzerland. Spain and several of its islands became a second home to me during the next few years.

Locations were specifically and logically chosen for us to experience unique energies of the land and homes within each region. Most classes lasted 12-14 hours each day and were three weeks long. We were steeped in these new-to-us energies, stayed in quaint villages, ate regional foods, talked with the local people, and absorbed the lessons being taught.

According to Dr. Maxwell Maltz in his 1960 book, *Psycho-Cybernetics*, it takes about 21 days for old mental habits to dissolve while forming new patterns. **Unbeknownst to us, we were changing our inner frequencies living in these energies for** three weeks. By the end of the immersion, we had absorbed these vibrations, resonating with them, and intuitively picked up on them when next exposed to them, no matter where that occurred. Our vibrational energies strike a chord when we come in contact with the same energy, bringing each into harmony.

The Face of Home

Children intuitively get energy and symbolism. Remember as a child how you drew a home? Most start with a square and an A-shaped roof, a door and two windows are added. They see animation in the inanimate. They sketch the "face" of a home with two eyes plus one large opening that's the nose-mouth combination.

Windows expand the feeling of space, connecting us to the world beyond and potentially allowing nature to become part of our environment. Sunlight enters brightening the space. Light, whether sunlight, moonlight or artificial light, enters our eyes enabling us to see. As humans, our eyes allow us to see an expansive world. Looking into another's eyes, we feel more connected.

In most Asian cultures, doors are known as the "mouth of chí." Doors let the chí, prana, life-force energy, or "breath of life," enter buildings.

Let's expand on the concept "breath of life" with the phrase, "A Breath of Fresh Air."

Anyone who's experienced a cold knows it's difficult to breathe through you nose. We open our mouth, take a deep breath, and fill our lungs with oxygen. This oxygen accelerates healing.

The FRONT door is considered the "main mouth of chi!" It allows bursts of fresh air to enter the home every time the door is opened. If you enter via a doorway connected to the garage, you aren't permitting "fresh" air to enter. You have second-hand air infiltrating your home, an air possibly containing carbon monoxide or chemical fumes from items kept in the garage.

If you enter through a back or side door, the chi may have difficulty finding that entrance. Generally speaking, the home's main entrance is seen from the street. If the chi has to make twists and turns to find your door, you lose direct vital energy desired in life. Hallway entrances, often found in condos and apartments, reduce even more fresh air and chi.

Since doors are linked to the mouth, they also represent communication. Not able to speak up? You may have a stuck door. As a speaker, my doors need to open wide for my voice to be heard worldwide. Hinges need to be oiled to prevent squeaking for my message to be taken seriously.

A strange term I learned was, "biting doors." These are doors that, when opened at the same time, hit each other. It often happens with closet or utility room doors and a main door to a room. I was amazed to find many of these households were homes of physical abuse. The correlation was uncanny!

Have you heard the phrase, "Eyes are the windows to the soul?" At night when the lights are on and the window coverings are open in a home, you can see inside. Looking deep into a person's eyes gives the sense you are looking into a person's Soul.

Then there is the whole "Give your home a facelift" to create the curb appeal attribute. Let's have fun with this one!

Give the front of the house a quick coat of paint (foundation), paint the front door (lip stick), polish the handles (brush the teeth), pull the weeds (make sure nothing is in between the teeth), paint the window shutters (eye liner and shadow), clean the windows (put on glasses or have clear vision), and caulk all cracks (hide the wrinkles).

The Home and Body Connection

I've mentioned several ways the body relates to the home: doors equal our mouth, windows equate to our eyes. In the various schools of Feng Shui, there are numerous correlations between the body and home. In my consultations I found if there were non-working doors, invariably one of the occupants had health issues with the mouth. Eye issues appeared when there were cracked or non-functioning windows.

There are many schools of Feng Shui. It is an intense, time-consuming process to delve deeply and thoroughly into all of them. Each connects the home and body in numerous ways, ways I've seen connected to health issues of the occupants, my clients! By **addressing the home problem we invariably improve the body's health.**

(As an exercise, think about this and see if you can find a connection between some current health issue and a corresponding aspect of your home.)

Here are a few more fun examples with body, home, and home accessory phrases or connections:

- House has good "bones" (framing)
- Building is losing its "footing" (foundation)
- Key is to "unlock" your mind
- Shades for your windows (sunglasses/shades for eyes)
- Teeth and tile (both made of porcelain)
- House Wrap (a plastic wrap placed around the home to keep wind and water out, just like a coat for your body)

Direct body associations used in the building industry:

- Butt joint
- Finger joints
- Hip joint
- Nails

Connecting Body, Mind, Spirit and Home

Having shared several ways that the body relates to the home philosophically, let's take it one step further. Sometimes the body is referred to as the "Temple of the Holy Spirit." Therefore, if our spirit lives in our body and our body lives in our home, doesn't our home deserve to be treated like a temple for our body and sSpirit–a scared temple filled with incredibly positive energy?

Take this in for a moment! Does your home FEEL like a temple? Is it a sacred place? Does it feel like a place where you can go to rejuvenate, rejoice, relax and recreate your life? Is it a place where you care for your body, the sacred temple that holds your sSpirit?

During my 50-year career I've observed something: in loved and cared for homes, life seems to go better for the occupants. If neglected, there are more issues in life—challenges about money, lack of loving relationships, disputes with children, health problems, career instability, or not feeling fulfilled with work, more struggles, more stress, fewer dreams come true, and far less fun enjoyed by the family!

Here are two acronyms guiding you to create better energy for your HOME and your SELF to empower self-care.

H.O.M.E.

H – Heal your Home: Natural cleaning products and furnishings support better indoor air quality, or oxygen, enhancing your vitality. Think of repairs as home "boo-boos." Band-aids work on some repairs, yet others require surgery to fix them.

O – Open Windows and Organize your home: Let fresh air fill your home as often as possible. Creating an orderly household removes stuck energy and helps you find things more easily freeing up time and energy.

M – Move furniture to create Movement: Arrange your furniture for easy traffic flow and functionality. Squeezing through tight areas restricts energy. And rather than straight thoroughfares, consider meandering pathways through the home for better flow.

E – Energize and Enrich your home: Bring in nature through flowers, plants, landscape artwork, statues, and photos of animals or birds. Play upbeat music and display crystals to raise the vibration in the home. Since color is vibration, add spots of it. Use essential oils to reduce mustiness and refresh the smells within the space.

S.E.L.F.

S – Sacred Spaces : Create spaces, even if they are hidden inside a dresser drawer, that feed your Soul, this is just for you. No one else needs to know about or see it! Altars and meditation rooms are mainstream home features and can produce balanced environments to soothe your Soul.

E – Essence of you: Who are you at your core? Nurture the discovery process by surrounding yourself with things you love. (Hint: Journaling and vision boards often help this self-discovery process). You may need a few functional items until you find the right piece and that's okay. Make a list of needed functions plus personal style for your desired feel in the space. **Don't be surprised when the PERFECT item shows up at the PERFECT price. The** Universe loves a focused mind and often manifests quickly. Remember, your home is your interior sanctuary.

L – Let your Light shine: You are a radiant spark of energy created to share your brilliance in the world. Do whatever it takes to make your home a castle filled with precious jewels reflecting your many facets of Love and Light.

F – Flow, Fantasy, and Fun: Don't take yourself seriously. Learn to flow with what comes in life; it's not happening TO you, it's happening FOR you! Life is designed to support you to become your best self – to grow and share your gifts. Create fantasy, whimsy, and fun moments whenever possible.

Your home interacts with you. It could be a place destroying dreams if you neglect it. Instead, give it love. **Nurture it. Show it how much you appreciate it for providing you with Maslow's basic needs of shelter, safety and security. Then, in return, your home will nurture you—your body, your mind, and your spirit.** After all, your home is a reflection of you, your essence, your hopes, and your dreams!!!

Linda Lenore

As one of the first non-Asian Feng Shui Masters in North America, a Certified Green Building Professional and Certified Vital Office/Home consultant (a European designation), Linda is known for creating corporate and home environments that stimulate success and soothe the soul as exemplified by some of her Feng Shui clients: Adobe Systems, Apple Computer, Bank of the West (SF Chinatown), First Republic Bank, and The Ritz-Carlton, as well as international media celebrities and royalty. With 60 years in the design industry, and 40 years of experience in Feng Shui, she's been featured as an expert in the *Wall Street Journal*, *Christian Science Monitor*, *San Jose Mercury News* (front page, 4/3/2000 "above-the-fold"), *Better Homes & Garden*, and several international syndications.

As a Feng Shui Master, she blends all schools of this ancient wisdom with interior and landscape design, Universal design, and green/sustainable building practices. Linda was recognized as an American Society of Interior Designers Distinguished Speaker and a University of California faculty member where she created the course "Green Feng Shui," the first course blending green/sustainable design-build practices with Feng Shui. A sought-after, award-winning university guest lecturer, keynote speaker, featured presenter at home and garden shows throughout North America, and featured in a European documentary on Feng Shui, Linda educates, motivates, inspires, and transforms her audiences. Her international best-selling book, *The Gift of the Red Envelope: A Guide to Designing Balance, Order and Beauty in Your Home* has been translated into several languages and printed in braille. Her amazing Hallmark Channel segment, Lifetime Media appearances, and presentations have inspired audiences through design, ancient wisdoms, and stories. Her television appearance on Voice AmericaTV instantly became the sixth most-popular program internationally. She does energy clearings, blesses environments, conducts courses and webinars, writes articles/blogs, and creates special events/retreats. She's known as "The Healing Designer!"

Email: **Linda@LindaLenore.com**
Phone: 360-768-4888
Website: **www.LindaLenore.com**
Facebook Personal: **https://www.facebook.com/linda.lenore/**
Facebook Business: **https://www.facebook.com/GreenChiDesigns/**
LinkedIn: **https://www.linkedin.com/in/lindalenore/**
Twitter handle: @LindaLenore88

EMBODY YOUR SENSUAL SELF
BY JILL ASHLEY HOFFMAN

It was after midnight. I was sitting on the ground in my dorm room during my second year of college and I was disgusted with myself for binge eating yet again. I was in so much physical pain but that didn't stop me. I didn't understand it at the time, but this was how I coped with the intense emotions I had been keeping bottled up inside.

My early childhood trauma taught me that my body was unsafe—just a storage facility for pain that I was committed to avoiding no matter what. Existing from the neck up, was not only a more preferable way to live but it was also more socially and culturally acceptable. Every day we are bombarded with messages that reinforce how NOT to feel worthy and trust our bodies. FAITH

Throughout my life, I abused my body with chronic dieting, over-exercising, not sleeping, self-mutilating, and compulsively binge eating. Deep down I didn't believe I was enough and that I didn't deserve to feel good. I was completely ignorant to the signals that my body was sending me, trying to get me to slow down. But I just kept going.

On the outside, I seemed ok. However, by the time I reached my early thirties, my body was starting to put on the breaks. I had a wonderful fiancé and my own business that was starting to gain momentum. Yet constantly hustling to validate my worth was completely taxing and draining my body.

Soon after getting married, I was diagnosed with adrenal fatigue and hypothyroidism. At one point, my cortisol (which helps measure adrenal function) was so low, it was practically off the charts.

I was tired all the time.

I had chronic constipation.

I experienced irregular menstrual cycles.

I gained almost 20 pounds in three months.

I was angry, confused, and completely overwhelmed. I didn't know anything about thyroid health at the time and my current doctor was not giving me a lot of solutions besides taking a pill for the rest of my life. So, I decided to take things into my own hands. I went back to school for health coaching. I was determined to heal my body naturally and toyed with the notion that I could help others do the same. This started me down my path of holistic healing.

Two years in, I was making progress with my health and even started coaching others to help them on their health journey. But to be honest I was still frustrated with myself. Even though I felt like I was doing everything right, my body was not making the progress I had hoped for. I was still struggling with my digestion and my weight and still felt at war with my body.

Something was missing. That "something" is what I now call embodying your sensual self.

Around three years into my holistic healing journey, I enrolled in a transformational coaching program which changed everything. I didn't really see it at the time, but the healing work I was doing in this program allowed me to return home to my body in a safe way by connecting to my sensuality.

I learned that sensuality is enjoying your body through your senses: sight, hearing, touching, tasting and smelling. I want to emphasize the *enjoying* part. Your senses are how you experience your body and the world, but most of the time we are too much in our heads to really enjoy our bodies and spend a lot of energy criticizing, judging, and negating our bodies. This is learned.

Babies are born loving their bodies. Did you ever see a baby feeling self-conscious about his/her leg rolls? Nope. Trust me, there was a time when you truly were comfortable, safe, and happy in your own skin. The world was your sensual playground and you couldn't wait to see, hear, taste, touch and feel EVERYTHING.

Then, one day something happened. Perhaps you were body-shamed. Perhaps you experienced trauma (physical, emotional, sexual, etc.) Or maybe you started off feeling safe in your body but then you got entrenched in the patriarchy, which diminishes the body. This wound has left people (especially women) feeling disconnected from their sensuality and ultimately burned out because this is not how we are designed to operate. This can lead to chronic health issues, poor body image, low self-confidence, and a total lack of energy.

Disconnecting with our sensuality is like saying "No" to life because your senses are the gift of being embodied in human form.

When you are disconnected from your sensuality, you might feel like something is missing and look to other outlets to fill that hole. Things like food, alcohol, work, sex, social media, TV can all seem like "normal" things to engage with on the outside, but can mask a feeling of deep dissatisfaction on the inside.

The truth is that we are all seeking our divine right to experience joy and pleasure in our bodies. We are wired for this more than anything.

Beauty in the world enlivens your sight and your ability to see.

Music and the sounds of nature stimulate your hearing.

Fresh flowers and the aroma of food bring you closer to your sense of smell.

Massage and taking warm luxurious baths will activate your sense of touch.

Chocolate, wine, and your favorite flavors stimulate your sense of taste.

Tapping into your sensual self will help you turn on the relaxation response, boost your immune system, increase your body confidence, help you heal old wounds, and connect you to your intuition.

Your intuition is your internal GPS because it's how you access your connection to your higher self. Your intuition is subtle, which is why you might struggle with hearing it but everyone has access to it—you just need practice connecting. That's where your senses come in!

This is how you restore trust with your body.

Why? Because this how you were born to be! Enlivened in your body, experiencing the world with your beautiful, activated senses!! You see, the body gets sourced and energized when we connect to our pleasure and sensuality, this is what lights up our creativity, intuition, and our natural inner-healing abilities!

The following are my favorite ways to embody the sensual self.

Deep Belly Breathing

What if I told you that you weren't just breathing in air, but that with every inhale you are breathing in healing light? Imagine that you could see, feel, smell, hear and even taste this light as it reaches every corner and crevice of your body. And with every breath, you have the opportunity to bring more balance to your mind, body, and soul. Would you pay more attention to your breath?

Most of us don't because breathing it is an autonomic process (YAY for not having to remember to breathe!). Consequently, mostly we tend to breathe shallow. Shallow breath keeps you in a fight-flight-freeze mode, which is the opposite of a healing state because it reinforces the stress and trauma of being at war with yourself.

The good news is that by intentionally practicing deep, slow belly breathing you can trick yourself into being relaxed. I mean, you're not really "tricking" your body, you're actually becoming relaxed when you breathe this way, but it can work so quickly that it's like hacking your nervous system.

Here's one method I really like that's simple: while sitting or lying comfortably, bring one or both hands to your belly. Close your eyes if that feels comfortable. Then, just start taking long deep breaths through your nose and feeling the air inflate your belly underneath your hand(s). Then, hold for 2 seconds and release your breath slowly through your mouth while your belly deflates underneath your hands. Start by practicing this for ten breaths and slowly increase this practice for up to 10-15 minutes.

See if you can extend your exhale longer than your inhale because this resets the nervous system. This will get easier over time, I promise. And, I also promise that if you practice this at least once a day you will notice a significant difference in your stress levels, energy, and creativity. You might just want to keep a journal nearby to capture any ideas that come to you while you are in your relaxation state.

Embodied Movement

Traditionally, we've been taught to move our bodies as a form of exercise. Exercise usually looks like running outside or on a treadmill, lifting weights, or taking a spin class. These are all fine ways to strengthen your body, but usually very masculine and goal-oriented.

Meaning, many people will push themselves to do these exercises because they desire a specific goal that exists in their head, but don't always check in with how their bodies feel or what their bodies need or want.

Embodied movement has no goal or agenda except to feel GOOD.

Why is this important?

Because when your body feels good, it feels safe. And, when your body feels safe, she can relax. And when your body truly relaxes, she can heal.

Most of us are starved for pleasure and for listening to what your body really needs. Embodied movement connects you to the energy and love that exists within your body, rather than trying to manipulate your body in some way.

Moving mindfully allows you to get out of your head and connect more deeply with your intuition because you're feeling instead of thinking.

My favorite way to connect to my sensuality through movement is dancing!

I believe that all women are dancers at heart. Whether you realize it or not, dancing is in your DNA. As a little girl, you probably pranced around to your favorite music without a care in the world about how you looked or what others were thinking. And, then at some point you stopped dancing. Maybe you can remember when that was or maybe not. It doesn't really matter. All that matters is that you can start again.

The cool thing is that the type of dancing I'm talking about requires no specific technique or dance step. All you need is music that inspires you to move and a little space.

Dance parties with others are awesome, but dancing solo allows a deeper level of safety and intimacy for your body to move how it truly wants to move. Allow yourself to really slow down in your movements and feel what it feels like to move your body in different ways.

Slowing down is key to connecting more deeply to your sensuality. I also recommend creating sacred space when you move this way. Light a candle. Maybe burn some incense. Find music that inspires your body to move naturally in a slow, sensual pace. Adorn your body with beautiful garments and accessories that make you feel sexy and alive.

By listening to how your body wants to move, you will start to rebuild trust with your body and connect to the wisdom that lives inside of you.

Connecting with Nature

Nature is high frequency life-force inside of you waiting to be activated.

So, then why are we all so tired?

I believe it's because as a species, we've become so disconnected with nature, physically and energetically. We've been distracted by conveniences of the modern world such as electricity, city living, fast food, and of course, our technological devices.

We've also forgotten that our rhythms correspond with nature's rhythms. You might have a hard time sleeping because your circadian rhythm is out of sync with the rising and falling of the sun. Or you might experience painful periods because you weren't taught that your monthly cycle follows the cycle of the moon.

Disconnecting with nature is very stressful on the body. Fortunately, reconnecting using your senses will greatly reduce stress, and allow your natural healing abilities to do their thing.

Here are some practical ways you can connect with nature on a daily basis:

Wake up early to enjoy a beautiful sunrise.

Open the windows to hear the birds chirping their song.

Take time to literally smell the roses (or whatever flowers are around).

Walk barefoot in the grass and connect to the healing power of the Earth.

Enjoy the taste of fresh herbs picked right from your local garden.

Nature is something we often take for granted. However, when we practice connecting to it in an intentional way, we are rebuilding that trust in our bodies because nature is our primary medicine.

Even if we live in a city or cold climate, there are many ways to connect with the healing power of nature. Biomimicry is a process of bringing the essence of nature into modern civilization and culture. Plants, crystals, essential oils, immersing in water, and even just lighting a candle are powerful ways to work with nature and to keep your home and body energetically alive.

There is a life-force within us that is craving to be heard. We have lost touch with our innate sensual self and I believe that this is one of the greatest causes of stress and dis-ease today.

I hope that the practices I have shared will help you meet that part of you yearning to be heard and trusted again.

- Deep belly breathing
- Embodied movement
- Connecting with nature

I am deliberately calling them *practices* and not tips because it takes consistency to regain trust with your body. Most of us have been disconnected from our bodies for years, if not decades, and so patience and compassion is paramount.

The good news is that the practices I've shared are relatively simple and low cost. All you need is an open mind and a commitment to creating time and space for exploring and re-engaging with your body in a new way.

What if you gifted yourself an extra 15 minutes in the morning and evening to dedicate to a sensuality practice of your choice for 21 days? You might light a candle and bring in your favorite music to make this time more pleasurable. This will make it even more powerful, I promise!

I would love to hear how you feel after you commit to embodying your sensual self for 21 days.

What have you discovered about yourself?

In what ways do you have a greater trust in your body?

How has your sensuality affected the way you experience the world?

I invite you to message me on Facebook or Instagram and let me know.

Jill Ashley Hoffman

Jill Ashley Hoffman is a Master Transformational Coach for empathic women who are ready to reclaim their energy and feel more confident, at peace, and FREE in their bodies. She helps them turn their tenderness into the medicine that heals their body so they can heal the world.

Since starting her coaching business over six years ago, Jill has worked with women on their health, body image, relationships, and spirituality. She soon realized that one of the biggest common denominators under-lying her clients' issues was that they were living very disconnected from their bodies and this was manifesting as disease in their life and keeping them from stepping into their true purpose.

Jill currently supports women on their *empowered healing* journey through live retreats, online events, and her private and group coaching programs, where she weaves in many modalities including re-imprinting and neuro-linguistic programming (NLP), food therapy, inner child work, breath work, and somatic practices such as, Kundalini yoga, embodied dance, chakra healing, oracle cards, and more.

Jill is also a Certified Integrative Nutrition Health Coach, Certified Transformational Life Coach, as well as a Certified Thyroid Health Coach. In her spare time, she loves to read, cook healthy meals for her and her husband, walk with her fur baby in the park, meditate, sing karaoke, and dance.

jill@jillashleyhoffman.com
jillashleyhoffman.com
https://www.facebook.com/jillashhoffman
https://www.linkedin.com/in/jillashleyhoffman/
@jillashleyhoff
https://www.youtube.com/channel/UCpFRLphT1QEX2MIegpGqYsg
https://www.instagram.com/embodymentor/

HEALING FROM WITHIN: TIPS FOR HEARING WHAT YOUR BODY AND INTUITION IS TELLING YOU
BY HEATHER LARKIN

I have to admit, my body made me do it. That's literally how I got into holistic healing and became a Reiki practitioner. It was also fundamental in creating my own business. As I started to accept that living in a state of frustration was normal and ignored the signs telling me otherwise, my body stepped in and forced me to listen. As the universe propelled me into similar situations time and time again, it finally helped me realize why it's so important to pay attention.

I say this with much love and advice I wish I'd taken sooner: do yourself a wonderful favor and pay attention to your body and senses! The more mindful you are, the more likely you are to embrace the challenges you face in life with greater appreciation and understanding. Tuning in to your own sense of self is incredibly empowering. Once you focus on *you*, and not the version you feel may be expected by everyone else, it will help break old patterns, create new ones, and essentially expose inherent tools to help you live your best life.

It is my hope that sharing my story and experiences will resonate with your own life journey. Please take comfort in knowing there's always an opportunity for transformation. All we need to do is stop and listen.

Tip #1: Listen to your gut and follow your instincts.

The first time I experienced what I now view as discernment was during my college years in Ohio. The campus was buzzing with students and collegiate activities. All around, lush trees surrounded the campus grounds, and breathtaking historical buildings drew attention with their varied architectural style from late Victorian, to mid-century modern.

I was accepted into the Conservatory of Music and among many creative and talented performers. Music filled the halls; I cherished the times when I'd walk around soaking in the sounds of lively instruments and angelic singing voices.

My music therapy courses were held at the conservatory. Looking around, I thought I was right where I belonged. I struggled with selecting my major and happy I made the decision to continue in music. I was doing something I loved while enjoying all these new experiences during my first weeks of school. *Or was I?*

Soon after these first few weeks, I noticed something wasn't right, and I was starting to feel it physically. I quickly developed ulcers, frequent panic attacks, and suffered from IBS that continued to intensify, all within my first year. After only a few months, I started doubting if I was really meant to be there.

Not only was I stressing about schoolwork and trying to be the perfect student, I had this nagging urge to keep questioning what I really wanted to do with my life.

Deep down I knew I was meant to do something beyond music, but couldn't figure out what it was, and it was driving me crazy. And then it occurred to me. Music was my creative outlet. I realized I was forcing it into something that wasn't for me. As soon as I tried to put structure around music and make it fit into a specific job or career, it backfired. I intuitively knew music therapy as a job was not going to happen during this particular time in my life.

Once I listened and stopped trying to do something I knew didn't feel right, everything shifted. I left the conservatory and switched to a major that would lead me to my career in marketing. I finally started listening to my instinct that I had been fighting to ignore.

Do you often listen to your intuition? How many times have you felt something wasn't right, but kept at it anyway? Many times, how we feel physically can be our biggest clue that we're not listening to what our higher self is trying to tell us. When you have a gut feeling about something, trust your intuition. It's always there to help.

Tip #2: Identify old patterns and form new ones.

Listening and trusting your instinct is one step of the process to self-empowerment. With this, we must also identify patterns and ways of changing old behavior.

Forming patterns can start as early as childhood and carry on throughout adulthood. Some of the ways we change old patterns and form new ones are done through self-awareness exercises and healing techniques. But before we get to that, let's first explore an example of what a pattern is and what behavioral signs look like.

Throughout college, my body was giving me signs to slow down, but I thought powering through was the only option. Even as a child, I displayed a pattern of striving for perfection. I just had this innate drive to succeed in everything I did, no matter if it made me feel downright miserable at times.

The cues I received in college varied, but the way in which they came on was consistent. I'd sit down to take an exam and slowly feel panic washing over me, my hands shaking and heart racing. Speaking in front of a group of people caused my throat to close up leaving me feeling embarrassed and frustrated. I would spend hours staring at pages of notes unable to concentrate, so I would isolate myself in a completely quiet room with absolutely no distractions.

The ongoing struggle of not being able to focus and fear of failure spiked tension headaches and stomach pains and certainly got my attention. Thankfully, this reoccurring pattern helped me to stop and think about what I was doing the moment I started to not feel well. I realized I was developing a pattern of believing that working hard equals discomfort. The more I trusted that belief, the harder it was to break the cycle.

Luckily, after seeing various doctors and specialists, I had the inclination to seek alternative methods of healing. This is when I was first introduced to Reiki and the chakra system.

From a holistic perspective, my chakras were off balance. Chakras are the energy centers within our bodies and keep the spiritual, mental, emotional, and physical health of the body balanced. For me, when I was under pressure my solar plexus would act up and my stomach would hurt and tighten. If I was too hard on myself, afraid to fail or not able to focus, my root and sacral chakra let me know by leaving me feel unmotivated yet worried about what I needed to accomplish. When I couldn't communicate effectively, avoided a tough conversation or speaking my truth on a matter, my throat chakra would close or trigger gagging when I spoke.

Using Reiki helped me to address my chakras and provided ways to relax and start learning to heal within. If you're not familiar with Reiki, here's a brief explanation of what it is and how it works:

Reiki is a Japanese technique that cleanses and balances the flow of energy in the body using universal life force energy. When a person's energy is strong and free flowing, the body and mind is in a positive state of health. However, when the energy is stagnate it becomes blocked or weak, and can lead to physical and emotional imbalance.

It's also important to know that the body has a natural ability to restore and generate physical and emotional well-being[1]. By activating the body's energy, Reiki breaks through to move these blocks, triggering the healing process.

My experience with Reiki was wonderful. I could feel waves of relaxation flow through my body. I was able to address aches and pains and calm my nerves in a way I never had before. Learning more about chakras in combination with Reiki helped create more awareness within my body and taught me the importance of creating balance. I found great benefit in using Reiki often and was amazed with the results. So much so, that I continued to study Reiki and became certified as a practitioner at the age of 20.

Just as you are evaluating the undesirable patterns you'd like to change, I encourage you to look at the positive patterns you've formed as

---

[1] International Center for Reiki Training, 2020

well. Appreciate your uniqueness and accomplishments and take time for self-discovery.

Wellness Assignment: A first step in self-discovery is to write a list of your accomplishments and put it someplace you will see it every day (on the wall, fridge, daily journal, etc.). This helps to not only recognize what brings you joy, but also creates a positive mindset that will result in positive actions.

In addition, create a daily gratitude journal. Write down what you're thankful for and all you have accomplished. Even the smallest thing counts. We all have the ability to wake up in the morning and set the tone for our day, and every day is a new opportunity to start modifying our actions and patterns.

Tip #3: Find strength.
Appreciate the self (yours and others).

When something becomes too difficult or motivation is lacking, understand that sometimes it's just due to fear and that's okay. Facing our fears is something we all need to do when we are going through our self-discovery process. From it, you get strength.

As you continue to work on recognizing what you've accomplished, record new challenges that come up. Notice how you feel physically and emotionally, and how you address these situations.

For example, after college I worked hard at creating my career path and achieved success within the field of marketing. About halfway into my career, I felt a strong pull back to the metaphysical and spiritual world. I tried to brush off the desire to learn more, as I didn't think I'd be accepted or taken seriously if I shared my beliefs. But the feeling didn't go away and I was continuing to notice changes within me.

My intuition and clairsentient abilities were getting stronger. Meaning, I could tune into the energy of a room and use my senses to instinctively feel out people and situations.

As an empath, I began to understand how I was using this ability as a benefit when working with people. I was becoming more self-aware of how I was impacting others and started paying closer attention to how one person's energy and attitude could change an entire conversation within minutes. As a manager, I was in position to coach my team and learned how to take elements of this awareness and apply it to their own job and daily interactions.

Now, I'm certainly not suggesting you have to be an empath or have psychic abilities to do this! My point is to recognize the fact that we all are unique. We all have our own gifts to share with the world. The more we appreciate ourselves and others as unique individual souls, the better we evolve as a collective and the more inspired we will feel to be our best selves.

Wellness Assignment: Take a moment to think about your unique skills and write them down. Are you a good listener? Do you love to write or create? Are you a good problem solver or have a special talent? Just because something comes naturally to you, doesn't mean it comes easily for everyone else. But because it's so normal for us to see our gifts as no big deal, taking time to list what you're good at—even if it feels minute—is going to help you become more self-aware.

Tip #4: Understand that the universe has got your back.

After college, I quickly shifted all my focus and energy into my career. With my self-confidence intact and a successful career in marketing, it seemed like everything was going well.

However, the universe was again giving me indications of what was to come. For years, I was presented with opportunities to create a new career path or incorporate healing into my everyday life. But I chose to ignore it, thinking moving up the corporate ladder and earning a high salary was more important in life; that is, until my early 30's, in which I not only became ill but suffered a life-changing injury as well.

It first began when the stress of a demanding job and starting a family became my entire focus. Over the course of a few years, my migraines and stomach issues had returned. In addition, shortly after the birth of my second child, I had a malignant tumor removed from my left breast that required reconstructive surgery. My body was giving me clear signs to do something about my mental and physical health, and the longer I ignored it, the more I received the opposite of a healthy mind, body, and spirit.

When my oldest daughter was four and my youngest at two, I was quickly moving up in responsibilities and landed a position I had dreamed about for years. This naturally added more stress, but I thought I could manage it all, even with my current ailments.

And then one Sunday morning, I fell full-force onto the edge of a wooden chest in my bedroom, the tip of my tailbone made contact, shooting excruciating pain up throughout my entire body. This tailbone injury led to chronic pain and three years of various ineffective treatments and medications.

I had fallen into old habits that didn't serve me. I wasn't listening to my intuition and those cues my body kept giving me. I was struggling to be a perfectionist; to be the ideal mother, wife, career women, boss, and so on. My ego was getting in the way of my natural intuition, which was telling me to slow down.

Then one day, after no longer being able to take the toll of emotional stress and physical pain, I knew it was time to make a change.

I had to start thinking about why I was doing this to myself and why it felt like there was no way but the hard way.

In doing so, I also realized I wasn't the only career women falling into this same pattern. It almost seemed expected and normal when I talked to fellow co-workers who were also trying to meet the demands of being a working mother.

I was on the go from the time I woke, until I went to bed at night. I had maybe an hour to myself during the day; I didn't take a lunch break. And it was clear that I, along with the women I talked to, were clearly not taking care of ourselves.

In my experience up to that point, working hard meant succeeding in life. I was helping to provide for my family. Pushing through each day meant I was strong and admirable. Having children and a high salary meant making sacrifices. I thought that is what you're supposed to do and it's just a part of life. But let me just say, feeling empowered to be you, taking time for yourself, and doing what is truly fulfilling is what's really important.

And so, I once again embraced what I seemed to have forgotten during my college years: I listened. I mean *really listened* to what my body and senses were telling me. And through a series of events and introductions to various people within the holistic healing and wellness industry, I turned to Reiki and prioritized self-care. I had to trust the universe and myself, taking a leap of faith without doubting my instincts and abilities to make a successful change.

In 2016, I left the corporate world and started working for myself as a marketing consultant. With more flexibility, I was able to get back into Reiki, music, and other healing modalities, which led me to create KC Holistic Healing.

I no longer have ongoing tailbone pain, my digestive issues have improved, my headaches have decreased, and I can address stress and anxiety simply by using Reiki. It's changed my life. Today, I can offer the understanding and guidance I received during my own journey. As an energy worker and consultant, I strive to encourage others to find their own self-empowerment and healing.

Tip #5: Put self-care and awareness into action

My primary clientele are women. Some are in a transitional phase or situation in which they are feeling stuck such as a job or relationship. Others are looking to try something new to help release old patterns, remove emotional blocks, or manage overall stress and physical pain.

Regardless of the initial reason they come to visit, there's one thing that's consistent: at some level, they recognize the signals their body and intuition is telling them. Even if they aren't fully aware, just taking the first step toward self-care creates an opportunity for change.

Making the decision to take time for yourself and saying yes to having something you really want is incredibly rewarding. It can be a goal, a change, a bad habit, or desired experience. Recognize that only you can take that first step to make this happen. Do something for yourself that you enjoy or try something new. It's your time and you need to take it!

Are you listening to your body, mind, and spirit? What are they telling you?

What I've learned from my experiences is that even though we are all on our own unique path, we are all part of the collective that impacts every being on earth. What we choose to do for ourselves as well for others impacts more than just one individual. Every day I'm reminded to say yes, to move forward, to be in the moment, to pause and reflect, to find balance and take time for self-care, to just listen. Once you decide to focus on your well-being in the most loving and authentic way, you are also making a difference in the lives of everyone around you.

For more information about Reiki and self-care, visit Heather Larkin at: **kcholistichealing.com**.

Heather Larkin

Heather Larkin is a ho̶   sion for helping people ach   better physically, e̶   Master with the I̶   moving from Clev   II certification i̶   Master certifi̶   Healing in K̶

Heath   cian. She att̶   ocus in musi̶   ting and bro̶   he oppor- tu̶   ise in areas   velopment are

                     Heather started her marke̶   d determined it was imperative   rated self-healing and energy therapy.   g is to apply her training and background in   g to each energy healing session. Having used k̶e̶   or herself, and seeing how

much it has changed her life, she now uses it to help others looking for alternative ways to heal and help achieve their wellness goals.

hlarkinkc@gmail.com
816-805-0587
kcholistichealing.com
Facebook: @kcholistichealing
facebook.com/kcholistichealing

ESCAPING THE WHIRLPOOL OF PAIN AND ADDICTION: TURNING I CAN'T INTO I CAN!
BY MARJORIE FAVUZZI

I was barely keeping my head from going under the whirlpool, struggling just to breathe. I was losing the battle. I feared that I would go under at any moment and, though I was terrified, I almost welcomed it. I was convinced that dying was the only way to escape this living hell.

I couldn't see any other way out. I had been living with soul crushing pain from fibromyalgia for ten years and it seemed that the only relief I got was from the opiates and many other narcotics I was taking. I truly believed I couldn't handle all the pain without them. My world had become very small. The drugs had become my closest friends, nobody else understood my pain.

I had undiagnosed pain for almost seven years before I found a doctor who knew about fibromyalgia and gave me the narcotic cocktail to cope. This ever-expanding need for more drugs continued for five years, until my doctor, who was also an addict, lost his license. I was referred to another doctor who was astounded that I could even stand upright while taking Vicodin, Valium, Soma, Ativan, Fastin, and Methadone around the clock.

Since a doctor gave all the pills to me, I couldn't be an addict, right? After all, with a husband, two beautiful kids, a dog, and a house with a picket fence, I didn't fit the stereotypical profile. I tried to give up just the Vicodin, but after having a very dark spiritual experience, I realized I couldn't do it on my own. I checked myself into a 28-day residential rehab center and confirmed that I definitely qualified as an addict.

The year was 1996 and it was very unusual for someone with chronic pain to come in for detox. The counselors wanted me to talk about getting loaded, but I had been on these medications for so long that I no longer identified with being intoxicated.

I was introduced to the 12 Step model from Narcotics Anonymous (NA). Sitting in an NA meeting, I heard the voice of addiction scream "Run, run, get out of here! If you stay here you will die!" I was terrified. Then a quieter voice said, "If you leave, you will die. If you stay, you might learn how to live, be a better mom, and save your marriage." That was the voice of reason, of truth, of God, and I was finally willing to listen.

The pain was intense, like the hounds of hell gnawing on my bones. I'd often hear the voice of addiction prodding me to leave, but I stuck it out for the sake of my family.

I completed treatment and returned home to an angry husband and two small children. The pain felt crushing and I wanted to jump out of my skin. I was a mess and my nerves were like a bunch of live wires, all sparking at once. I was emotionally reactive and felt hollow, as if a giant cannon ball had gone right through me.

What I didn't know then was that the real physical pain in my body was amplified by my painful childhood experiences of sexual, mental, and emotional abuse. My subconscious had held the memories, and they were rising to the surface. I no longer had the drugs to numb them.

I attended NA meetings and I was told that, according to statistics, up to 85% of us would relapse in the first year and only one would still be clean in five years. I swore that I'd beat the odds and stay clean.

My husband and I were still fighting. I knew I couldn't stay clean if we didn't get help. We got into couples therapy, but it was rough. Our tenth anniversary was coming up. Friends loaned us their cabin and left us champagne. I was six months clean and heard God's voice say "you shouldn't have any," but I took a gulp. I started to feel relaxed and heard "it's okay, have some more, everything will be alright." I recognized that seductive voice of addiction, the invisible hand that was beckoning me. I ran to the sink and poured it out, feeling like I had just stuck my toe into the whirlpool again. Despite all my resolve to stay clean and sober, I had become a statistic of relapse.

The feelings were too intense. I had no other tools. Sugar became my next drug and I gained 65 pounds in the first ten months of recovery. I was now a "double-winner" in NA and Overeaters Anonymous (OA). I worked the 12 Steps with a sponsor, and the "God-sized hole" in me started to be filled. I stayed clean and sober long enough to discover better ways to overcome pain, release the weight and enjoy life.

If this all sounds a bit extreme, it's more common than you know. Though moderate use of pain medication is appropriate after surgery, many people fall into the web of addiction. Intending to use the opiates for only a short time, they find themselves unable to live without the narcotics that are intentionally manufactured to become addicting. Even after getting off of them, the statistics of staying clean without support is low. Some may resort to using street drugs to feed the need and drug overdose is the leading cause of accidental death in the United States, with opioids being the most common drug. - **https://pubmed.ncbi.nlm.nih.gov/29262202/**

The chances of living with pain and staying clean are much higher if the underlying trauma and anxiety is cleared. I have experienced and seen that this often shifts and lowers pain. Though I've now had fibromyalgia for 35 years, I practice acceptance and honestly have *much* less pain now than when I was taking all the narcotics 25 years ago.

If I knew then what I know now, it could have been so much easier. The key to real relief came when I learned the healing techniques I still use today. When pain arises, I breathe into it with compassion and allow it to soften. I use the Emotional Freedom Technique™ (EFT) of tapping on energy meridians and acupressure points to release emotions and trauma. I also ground and focus in the present moment with PACE from Brain Gym™. These simple exercises are an integral part of my self-care. I remember that this too shall pass and I recognize that, in this moment, I am relatively safe and well.

Here are some stories of clients who continue to triumph over pain while in recovery:

Maryanne

Maryanne had been hit by a car while walking across a street and had a lot of residual pain. She was receiving physical therapy, but her pain was as much emotional and mental as physical. She had Attention Deficit Hyperactivity Disorder (ADHD) and had been told that she could never do anything right as a child. She didn't feel worthy of success or happiness. Any sense of self-esteem came from giving away her time and energy to care for others. She didn't even realize that she wasn't practicing self-care until she learned how to stop doing so much for others and focus on her own needs.

The pain management tools and process I shared with her allowed her racing thoughts to calm down so she could better manage stress. The pain became much more tolerable. Tapping unlocked patterns that she had been stuck in, and she realized that she had outgrown her old sense of self. She set boundaries of time with family and realized that, when she took care of herself, she got more respect. Maryanne trained to become a Medical Assistant and now has been clean and sober for seven years.

Jeri

Jeri had been in recovery for five years and had recently been forced to leave an abusive job where she'd been screamed at repeatedly. She had worked the 12 Steps of Alcoholics Anonymous (AA) but was still filled with shame, anxiety, and low self-esteem. She also had chronic back pain and anxiety. She had abused opiates in the past. She said her self-esteem was in the toilet and she felt beaten down. We did EFT tapping to clear the Post Traumatic Stress Disorder (PTSD), and she gained a new sense of confidence and strength. After working together, Jeri said that she could truthfully say I *deeply love and accept myself.* She found the modalities transformational and very solution oriented. Jeri now has 25 years clean and sober and manages her back pain through tapping, PACE, and acupuncture.

Delilah

Delilah was a methamphetamines addict in recovery who had become a food addict after getting clean. She held trauma from being bullied for being overweight her whole life, before she found methamphetamines to keep her skinny. She didn't want to slip back into using the drug but hated her body. She had anxiety and pain in her back and legs. She had tried dieting, but binged on sugar and gained back the original weight, plus more. She was working long hours and said she didn't have time to take care of herself, but the panic of seeing her weight increase was horrifying. Finally she felt defeated and the fear of relapsing brought her to the point of surrender. She was ready for change.

Through tapping, Delilah escaped the rut of compulsive eating by creating new pathways in the brain and realizing that she was worthy of self-care. She resolved core issues around food and no longer allowed her defiant inner child to overeat. She had a complete shift in thinking and now enjoys working out daily. Delilah now has three years clean and sober, her body is stronger, and the pain is gone. She is grateful for the amazing transformation.

Reeducate Your Brain to Let Go of the Past and Ease Your Pain

Today I have 25 years clean and sober with a lower level of pain. My life is full of light, love, and purpose. I am a Certified Life Coach, Brain Gym Instructor, EFT and Matrix Reimprinting Practitioner. As the CEO of Success In Hand, I created the system Turning I Can't Into I CAN!® to help those with pain release it and learn that they are worthy of so much more. Seeing clients soar into the bright possibilities of a life, full of hope in recovery, brings me such joy.

To support you in letting go of the past and easing your pain, I want to give you these exercises:

Try them for one week and let me know how they work for you. You can contact me at **Marjorie@SuccessInHand.com**.

⌂ PACE from Brain Gym

This ten-minute exercise calms swirling thoughts and soothes the fight, flight, freeze response to bring you right into the moment. It's great for focusing, learning, and making good decisions. To do it along with me go to: **PACE Exercises with Marjorie Favuzzi** on YouTube.

⌂ The Emotional Freedom Technique (EFT), also known as Tapping

EFT is a technique of tapping the energy meridians of the body to access the pre-verbal parts of the brain. It's very effective for overcoming PTSD, anxiety, shame, resentment, and pain. Faster than talk therapy, it helps to neutralize emotions, clear trauma, and create new pathways in the brain that align with who you want to be today. Try the sample script below. Share your results with me by emailing **Marjorie@SuccessInHand. com**.

An EFT Script of Tapping to Release Anxiety and Pain

When you use EFT on these feelings and experiences, a cognitive shift takes place. Your level of distress decreases and dissipates as you acknowledge the pain and issues, bringing more ease and the ability to move forward.

- Choose ONE issue to tap on.
- Check in to see how much distress/anxiety you're feeling about this particular issue. Rate the Subjective Unit of Distress (SUD) on a 1-10 scale, with 10 being the highest.
- Begin tapping, using the script below, *customizing the words to fit your needs.*
- After tapping for two complete rounds, check in again to assess your SUD level. Continue tapping, adding in your own words as the emotions and pain decrease.
- Start doing a positive round when your SUD level is around 2.

Tapping Script – use this or substitute your own words!

Karate Chop Point (outside edge of the hand): *Even though I feel pain, I accept myself, just as I am.*

Karate Chop Point: *Even though I'm anxious, I accept myself, just as I am.*

Karate Chop: *Even though I'm hurting, I accept myself, just as I am.*

Top of Head: *Can I live with this pain?*

Between the Eyebrows: *This anxiety is paralyzing...*

Side of Eye: *I can't focus...*

Under Eye: *Why me?...*

Under Nose: *I shouldn't have to...*

Under Lip: *I need relief . . .*

Under Collarbone: *I don't want to feel this way...*

Under Arm: *Nobody understands...*

Top of Wrist: *These feelings are too much*

Underside of Wrist: *I don't know if I can do this*

Repeat as many times as needed, changing the words as you need to, until you have lowered the anxiety to level 2 or 3.

Positive Round – Use this or substitute your own words!

Top of Head: *I have this new tool . . .*

Eyebrow: *I can reach out for support...*

Side of Eye: *Stay focused on self-care...*

Under Eye: *I'm letting go of the anxiety*

Under Nose: *It'll feel so good to overcome this...*

Under Lip: *I'm breathing into the pain...*

Under Collarbone: *Allowing it to soften...*

Under Arm: *I let go...*

Top of Wrist: *I release this anxiety . . .*

Underside of Wrist: *I want to stay clean*

Top of Head: *I'm open to doing well...*

Eyebrow: *I'm present*

Side of Eye: *I release any anxiety in my body...*

Under Eye: *I breathe into the pain...*

Under Nose: *This too shall pass...*

Under Lip: *I am safe . . .*

Collarbone: *I can stay clean...*

Under Arm: *I release any frustration and overwhelm in my body...*

Top of Wrist: *I release this anxiety . . .*

Underside of Wrist: *Letting it all go . . .*

These are simple exercises that really work however, for deeper issues, working with a practitioner can yield deeper lasting results. Let me know how it works for you. To see how this will benefit you, visit **www.SuccessInHand.com** and book a free 30-minute consultation.

Please note: Although pain medications are appropriate after surgery, many people get immediately addicted. Reach out for support. There is an easier, softer way to lessen the multi-layered pain and live a life of being happy, joyous, and free. You and your loved ones deserve that.

Marjorie Favuzzi

Marjorie Favuzzi has lived with chronic pain for more than 30 years. Twenty-five years ago she rejected the destructive path of addiction to prescription pain killers and found EFT, a better way to live an expansive, fulfilling life. Marjorie is trained in the Emotional Freedom Technique, a method based on ancient wisdom to release trauma, calm emotions, and relieve physical pain. As the CEO of Success In Hand, Marjorie teaches her signature system, Turning I Can't Into I CAN!® internationally through workshops, groups and individual sessions. Contact Marjorie to move beyond your challenges and regain a higher quality of life. You, too, deserve to have Success In Hand.

Certified Life Coach, EFT & Matrix Reimprinting
Practitioner, Author, and Speaker
ISP State of California, Dept. of Rehabilitation
707-206-1477
Website: **www.successinhand.com**
Facebook: **https://www.facebook.com/SuccessinHandToday/**

A LIFE WITHOUT MIGRAINES
BY DR. PAULA STRAUSS

"That no one dies of migraine seems,
to someone deep into an attack, an ambiguous blessing."
– Joan Didion

What is the most important thing to place in a migraineur's ear? Words of comfort. That is what patients with migraines need more than any-thing. For those of us who do not have severe, painful migraines, we must understand that it is disabling and there is no solution as of yet. The best medicine has to offer is that 50% of patients respond (a little or a lot) to any given medication. The other 50% is left to manage and cope on their own. I have attended many seminars with migraine advocates who are also experiencing migraines, and this is their overwhelming wish—to be heard, to be recognized, to have it understood that this is a major, life-affecting problem. That alone would be a great help. Most people with migraines are tired of hearing suggestions of what to do, commiseration about their own headaches (which don't compare), and encouragement to soldier on. It would be better to offer simple acknowledgement and support, such as asking "what can I do for you?" or "what can I get you that will help?" or "go home, I will cover for you," to name some examples. Just being there for the migraine sufferer is immensely helpful.

My Story

I became a chiropractor as a second career. I had always thought of becoming one since I was a little girl and had my neck adjusted by our grumpy, old fashioned, small town chiropractor. I was thrilled to find out that I had a talent for adjusting! In chiropractic school, I was drawn to the most proof oriented, scientific methods available and I was wildly lucky to find a mentor who could lead me to that technique of chiropractic. I became an Upper Cervical (upper neck) specialist using diagnostic imaging to see changes in nerve function due to my adjustments.

As I began to practice in 1996, I noticed that my migraine patients improved with my treatment, although they usually came to me with a more traditional case of neck or back pain. I started to wonder if my work in the upper neck could have a significant effect on eliminating migraines. My own husband suffered from migraines and I had to stand by helplessly as he went through these terribly painful events, in the dark, alone. He was also under my care and he remarked to me one day that he had not filled his prescription for Imitrix in months and couldn't really recall his last migraine.

I made the shocking realization that the upper cervical treatment could provide migraine elimination, not just relief in a form of a pill or shot, just not prevention (if caught in time but not reliably), but actual elimination of the migraines my patients were having. And I made another shocking discovery: there was no treatment available to migraine patients that was drug-free. This was a totally unknown solution.

I got really, really excited! I focused my practice on migraine treatment. Now I see many migraine and other headache patients using this therapy. There are migraine patients out there, as I am sure you know, who do not respond to drug therapy, who are too sensitive for drug therapy, who go to the ER with terrible pain, and who are losing hope and are being drained of life because of their migraines.

My greatest hope and aspiration is to bring this treatment into the body of treatments available for migraine patients. I don't know if it is possible because the medical community remains hostile and doubting of the efficacy of chiropractic treatment, even after over 150 years of chiropractic doctors showing that a patient could crawl in and walk out of their offices. When I talk to my patients, they constantly reiterate that they are so happy to have their lives back, to not depend on drugs, and to not fear every vacation, wedding, graduation, project that could be ruined by a migraine. These patients have a been the source of my enthusiasm and joy for more than 20 years.

This chapter discusses that things that you, the migraine sufferer, have at your disposal to manage and reduce your headaches. Although many chiropractors claim to treat headaches, and they do have some success, the upper neck gives us access to those powerful nerve signals that can cure migraines if allowed to heal. You must seek out an upper cervical doctor to have a chance at this type of relief. I wish you all the best health in your migraine journey.

This is a treatment you have not heard about yet that uses no drugs, is not a pill, and over time, actually reduces the frequency, intensity, and duration of your migraines. It is not painful, it is safe, and better than 95% of patients can tolerate it. However, it takes time. With time, your migraines fade and stop.

CERVICAL VERTEBRAE

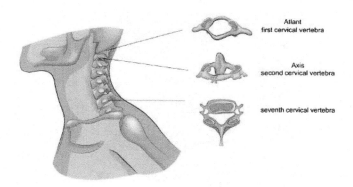

Atlant
first cervical vertebra

Axis
second cervical vertebra

seventh cervical vertebra

Start with the idea that the brain AND nervous system control all the functions in your body. These two related systems handle the functions that occur in your body. The nervous system has different parts in addition to your brain and one of them is called the brainstem. The brainstem has special nerve cells embedded in it that control lots of things in your head, like vision, hearing, balance, sensation of the face, and pain. These systems are affected by migraines.

Think of all the things that have happened you in life: maybe a difficult birth, falls from your bike, years of gymnastics, hockey or football, years of sitting to study in poor posture. These are the things that knock your top two bones of your neck out of place and put physical pressure on the brainstem. And suddenly you have migraines. Fixing the alignment of top two bones involves super gentle neck adjustments. Many people are afraid of adjustments. Once you see a ninja twist the head of their target and hear the crunching noise on a movie, you cannot un-see that. This approach does not include a ninja adjustment to the neck, but a gentle tapping instrument that is better suited to make small precise corrections, without twisting or turning the head.

Two things make this a breakthrough treatment. 1) Monitoring of the nervous system with a non-invasive scanning tool. 2) Soft, easy-to-take treatment that has many variations to help the many different body types and physiologies that have migraines.

The monitoring tool is called infrared thermography. This non-invasive tool scans your neck temperature looking for abnormal heat patterns. Over time, you will see your abnormal scan become normal. After one month, migraines become less often, less painful and shorter.

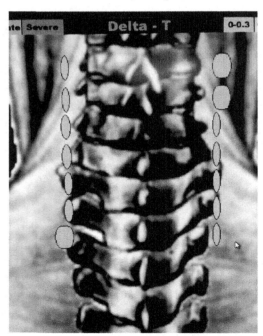

Infrared thermography scan: normal

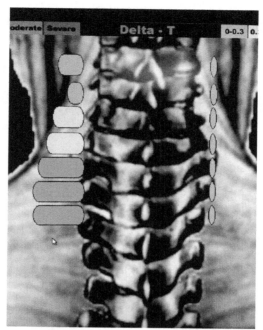

Infrared thermography scan: abnormal

According to your brain, as a migraine patient, you are a hot mess of wasted energy that could be used for other things, not only body functions, but life functions. When your migraine hits, it fires your weak spots like labored breathing, no concentration, too much sensation, squirrelly vision, and all of those things waste your energy. Your brain uses the treatment to reorganize the firing of neurons, so they do not produce the headache (which is very wasteful). Your normal, efficient state is to NOT produce a headache every time you drive at night, drink too little water, work in the sun, etc. As your brain learns to take the normal pathway over and over again, you experience less migraines and have a much more robust brain controlling all your body functions.

It's important to note, your migraine nerve pathway has not been eliminated. You can still trigger that pathway with all the usual factors: dehydration, overexposure to heat and light, driving at night with flickering lights, missing meals, too much alcohol, certain foods and so on. You must still be vigilant and aware of what you are doing. But the upside is that you might be able to tolerate some of the things you miss, such as chocolate, red wine, orange juice, and the beach for example. One of the biggest upsides of this treatment is that keeps your body functioning at its best. You can keep your mental and physical functions at a high level by having periodic adjustments to the neck and nervous system.

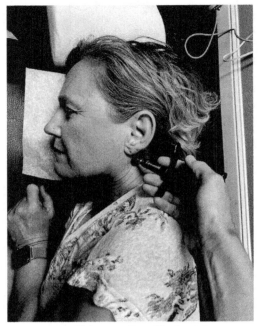

Chiropractic adjustment

I can diagnose you, support you, and treat you, but for times when you are at home, at night, on vacation, on work trips etc., you still need drugs to help you manage your situation. At this time, management is all you have and medical science has developed many management tools in pill form.

There has been a great increase in prescription medications that are swallowed, injected, inhaled, and taken only once per month. There has been good scientific progress in the last few years. These new drugs are promising, and some are on the market now.

If you do not want to take medications, there are natural herbs and supplements that might help. This is my most current and best list: magnesium, Vitamin D3, CoQ10, Vitamin B2 (Riboflavin), Feverfew, Butterbur, CBD, Vitamin D3, Melatonin.

There are two types of people: those that choose the "kitchen sink" approach of trying many new things at once, and those who want to know what works. Here are a few things that I think work for most people, as well as some that have had varied results:

Magnesium (without calcium) supplements

Many studies have been done showing decent results. As with all supplements, you need an excellent quality supplement made by a reputable company. Most doctors can order one for you that has been tested for quality.

Vitamin D3

Again, many studies have shown that Vitamin D3, especially in the world where we work indoors, and if you live at a latitude where the sun is not as strong, helps with a myriad of symptoms including migraine. Vitamin D3 is more absorbable than just Vitamin D.

Feverfew, Butterbur

These two herbal supplements that have varying success for patients.

Melatonin

Use melatonin as a sleep aid since sleep problems are often associated with triggering migraines, Use melatonin to get better rest and sleep. More is not better! Too much melatonin will interrupt sleep cycles.

Other natural approaches:

Colored glasses (rose, blue or green)

Unbelievably, colored glasses reduce the triggering effect of light. They can be bought online or you can ask your optometrist to make them for you. Most recently, green light exposure has been used to reduce migraine in patients that have many, many migraines per month. The rose color was the first color cited as helpful.

Marijuana (solution or capsules)

Marijuana had been used for centuries for headache treatment until it was outlawed in the 1930s. Scientists have found that marijuana works with your body's naturally occurring endocannabinoid system and has positive neurologic effects particularly on the trigeminal nerve (implicated as a source of migraine neurology). CBD mixed with THC can be used as a sleep aid as well.

Coenzyme Q10

Studies have been done to show the effectiveness of C0Q10, but results for patients are mixed. Your body makes it naturally and it is regarded safe.

Riboflavin or Vitamin B2

B vitamins are recognized as better used when taken as a group rather than one at a time, but in this case, I would make the exception to use this alone. Results vary.

Breath control

There are many apps to help you take deep breathes and it serves two good functions. When in a migraine, it gives you the focus point for your mind, helping you feel less pain and relax, which will help you sleep. Breathing exercises are especially good for kids to give them control over their migraines and pregnant women who do not want to use medications.

Meditation

There are many apps, YouTube classes, and in-person classes to help you meditate. I believe that meditation can be done for one minute, five minutes, or longer, and still benefit you. This is a practice to avoid triggering a migraine. Great for kids who learn the skill easily.

Self-hypnosis

Like meditation, self-hypnosis could be used in a migraine to distract from pain and help bring you into sleep. You may not want to hear anything because sound is so acute during a migraine, but this is also a good prevention technique that gives your brain the suggestion to suppress the migraine. Kids learn self-hypnosis easily.

Acupuncture

Western medicine has studied acupuncture and found that it is excellent at pain control. Acupuncture for a migraine in progress might be helpful for some. Results are mixed on their ability to prevent migraine.

Muscular pain reduction techniques

If your migraine comes with neck pain, you can learn trigger point therapy for the neck and shoulders. It is easy to do and lots of great tools are on the market to help you. Not all patients know if they have trigger points that contribute to their headache. A chiropractor, massage therapist, or physical therapist can tell you if you have them or not. I regularly do trigger point therapy on patients to improve their migraine relief and I teach them how to do it at home.

Migraine treatment is advancing with many interested doctors and advocates pushing for more treatment development. Chiropractic treatment is something amazing to offer you that medicine cannot: fixing the root cause of the problem–a faulty operating nervous system. Taken with all your other tools, your migraines become a manageable problem instead of a constant source of pain and anxiety. I wish you well with your journey to reduce and end your migraines.

Paula Strauss, D.C.
The Headache Doctor of Campbell

Dr. Paula Strauss has been in chiropractic practice in the South Bay since 1996. She earned a Bachelor of Science degree in Environmental Science and a Doctorate of Chiropractic from Palmer College of Chiropractic. Dr. Strauss specializes in migraine relief using Upper Cervical chiropractic treatment combined with manual therapy, exercises, and life style modification.

Dr. Strauss' mission is to offer a truly conservative, safe, drug-free migraine treatment to the thousands of migraine suffers in Silicon Valley where she practices and the greater world. The number one concern of her patients is that ongoing drug therapy will have long term, harmful health effects. Patients realize that drug therapy is not a cure of any kind, but only masks the symptoms until the next headache occurs. These people are wishing for a solution that actually reduces or eliminates the number of headaches they have and Dr. Strauss offers a unique treatment that does exactly that.

www.theheadachedoctor.com
Facebook: The Headache Doctor of Campbell Chiropractic
dr@theheadachedoctor.com

YOUR BODY'S INNER WISDOM: ILLUMINATING THE CELLS AND THE CRANIOSACRAL STORY
BY ILANI KOPIECKI

Have you ever wondered how the body heals? How does it mend a cut or bruise without anyone telling it what to do? How can it transform trauma and fright into inner peace and harmony? In Craniosacral Therapy we call this miraculous process the body's inner wisdom. It is a deep self-healing mechanism wired into every human being. In treatment sessions, I have experienced inner wisdom helping clients (and myself) release and unwind from the body's physical, mental, and emotional issues. The following treatment stories will help to illustrate the inner wisdom's amazing healing power. All names are fictitious to ensure client privacy.

Bill stumbled into my office being held by his sister Jenny, his eyes full of confusion and fright. He had never received a Craniosacral treatment and was full of doubt. Jenny was a long-time client and she brought him to me hoping I could help. Bill accepted the appointment because he was desperate. Up until a couple months before, he drove trucks in the North Dakota oil field but had lost his job due to a terrible accident. He had just arrived at the field station to end his shift for the day. It was mid-winter, and the ground was frozen solid. Bill opened the cab door and started to climb down the icy steps. He slipped and fell six feet, landing on the rock-hard roadway, hitting the back of his head. He suffered a severe concussion, and ever since that day he experienced blurry vision out of his left eye. As a result, his depth perception was affected and he couldn't even walk in a straight line, let alone keep his trucking job. He had been to numerous doctors with no relief other than being prescribed anti-depression medication.

After listening to his story, I asked Bill to lie down on the treatment table. Using my Craniosacral assessment skills, my hands listened very carefully to what his body's tissues were telling me. The most profound issue was that his sphenoid bone (the cranial bone behind the eyes) was severely impaired. The only word to describe it was "stuck." I gently worked with Bill's sphenoid to help release the tight tissues surrounding it. It just didn't want to release. I then had an idea: invite Bill to communicate directly with his body. In Craniosacral Therapy we call it accessing the body's inner wisdom.

I quietly asked Bill to take a deep breath and ask his body where to go to help his eye heal. After a few moments he slowly raised his hand and pointed to his left temple. "It's way inside," he said. His body's inner wisdom was telling him where to go! I grabbed a model of the cranium off the shelf and showed it to him. Without any hesitation at all he pointed to the left-hand bottom part of the sphenoid, which is attached by a joint to the upper mandible (the bone right below the nose that holds the upper teeth and roof of the mouth). So, with this knowledge, I slowly and gently started releasing the sphenoid from the upper mandible. At some point in the procedure we both heard a loud pop. Bill took a deep sigh and said that he felt something release inside his head.

We finished up the session and I invited Bill to sit up. He slowly opened his eyes and looked around. To his great excitement he could see perfectly through his left eye! His left optic nerve had been pinched by the stuck sphenoid, and now it was free. It just took Bill a moment of deep listening to his body to access the answer we needed. Later I found out that he was able to quit his medication and was re-hired at his truck driving job. Thank you, inner wisdom!

The body's inner wisdom can help in the healing process in so many ways. I have a personal story to share about the inner wisdom helping me with a very old trauma. I was attending a week-long advanced Craniosacral class. Every day, teams of five would work with each other, with four people giving and one person receiving treatment. On the third day, during my session, something amazing happened. With four loving and experienced hands holding the space for my self-healing journey, I spontaneously experienced my own birth. The scene just appeared behind my closed eyes, and unfolded like a long-forgotten story. I felt warm and comfortable in my mother's womb, then I was moving through a tunnel into bright light. I felt the shock of cold air on me. My stomach was nauseous from the gas my mother and I had received. I was aware of lots of activity around me and I became very confused. I wanted to hear my mother's voice and feel her touch, but she was sedated from the gas and couldn't move or talk very well. I wanted to see my father and sisters, but they were not allowed into the room. I thought, "Where is my welcoming party?" No one thought to hold me, talk to me, or make me feel safe. The medical team was busy bustling around me with their various jobs. I felt so alone and scared.

The Craniosacral team helped me move through the trauma. I felt the fear and sorrow literally drain from the tissues in my body. I became very relaxed and still, breathing deeply. It was as if the cells themselves held that memory (Craniosacral practitioners call this phenomenon cellular memory), and when they fully released, all that was left was pure light. I know now that my body's inner wisdom directed that healing session. By some miracle, it knew that it was the appropriate time for me to re-live, release, and integrate that experience. I am forever grateful for that precious gift. It started me on a path of deeper self-discovery.

Inner wisdom can also help people through a healing method called body talk. I want to share a remote healing session I gave using this process. Camilla called me to set up a Zoom session. She was suffering from discomfort that radiated from her left shoulder joint into her neck. She had tried various other treatments, but nothing seemed to work for very long. I arranged a time to meet on Zoom. During the session, I asked her to lie down on her couch, set up the webcam so I could see her, and get comfortable. Then, using Craniosacral Therapy technique, I energetically scanned her body, asking it to show me any and all reasons her shoulder and neck were not healing. Through reading the body's cranial rhythm, the body pointed to a tissue attachment in her shoulder joint. It had been pulled, and it seemed like a very old injury that never fully healed. Camilla shared with me that she had problems with that shoulder for many years. I asked her what was happening in her life when the pain started to appear. She remembered it was when her child was very young, and her life was very stressful. She was having marital problems, and she felt totally responsible for her family and the finances. She remembered holding the baby on her left hip for long stretches of time as she did housework. Then she began having issues with her shoulder and neck. I asked her to put her attention deep into her shoulder, where the tissue was pulled. When she had a clear picture, I invited her to talk to the tissue, as if it were a close friend, and ask it why it got pulled and why it didn't heal. After a long silence the words came, "too much weight." I asked Camilla what that meant. She thought it meant that she took on too much responsibility for other people. Then she realized that the tissue was pulled because of the emotional and physical weight she carried for others in her life.

By using body talk and deeply listening, Camilla understood the source of her pain and discomfort. Her body's inner wisdom was given a voice! We set up a plan where she would totally rest her shoulder for a couple of weeks. I also asked her to consider giving up some areas of work in her life so others could take on more responsibilities. Camilla's inner wisdom guided her to the source of her physical problem and helped her to make some healthy lifestyle changes.

Each of us is gifted with a wonderful inner wisdom that can help us understand how to help our body self-heal. All that is needed from you is a willingness to slow down, listen, and receive guidance from that voice within. It is just waiting to communicate with you! Why does this process work? How can it know the right timing to give us information? Why is it even there at all? I have no answers for you. I like to think that Divine Source knows the right timing and setting to guide us into optimal health. What I do know is that the body is miraculous, and its deepest urge is to come into healing balance so that all of our cells are illuminated with healing light.

The following meditation is a gift for you to get in touch with your own inner healing power.

Accessing Your Body's Inner Wisdom Meditation

I invite you to have someone read this meditation to you. Or you can record it yourself, speaking slowly and clearly, pausing in between directions. Try using this meditation 2-3 times a week, so that you become familiar with tuning into your body's inner wisdom.

A couple suggestions before you begin:

- Find a time when you can be quiet and undisturbed for 10-15 minutes.
- Turn off your phone.
- Settle your pets.
- Keep a notebook and pen handy to jot down thoughts later.
- Sit comfortably in a chair, feet flat and hands resting face down on your thighs.
- Plan to sit quietly for a few minutes after the meditation, so you can write down a few notes and fully integrate the experience.
- Think of an area in your body that needs attention.

The Meditation:

Gently close your eyes. Take a few deep, slow breaths, inhaling through your nose, then slowly exhaling out your mouth. Feel yourself relaxing and sinking into your chair. Just let yourself go and allow the chair to hold you up. When you are ready, put your attention on an area in your body that is calling out to you. Gently give it your loving attention. Talk to it like a very close friend. With deep compassion and love, respectfully ask why it is at unrest. Keep breathing slowly, and wait patiently. Continue to give the area your loving attention. Feel yourself opening to your body's inner wisdom and its healing message. The answer may come as words, images, or body sensations. If you don't understand the message, respectfully ask the question once again. The message may come again in another form. When you are ready, lovingly ask your body what you can do to help this area heal. Breathe deeply and wait patiently, knowing your inner wisdom is finding its voice to give you an answer. When you feel your process is complete, give gratitude to your inner wisdom for all its help. Sit quietly for a few moments. And when you are ready, gently open your eyes.

Afterwards:

- Check in with your body. How does it feel?
- Check in with your feelings. Is anything coming up? If so, breathe fully and let it go.
- Jot down any messages you may have received during the session.
- Drink some water to refresh yourself.
- Give yourself a big hug for entering into your self-healing journey!
- You can also access my audio recording of this meditation by following this link to my website: **ilanisessions.com**

Ilani Kopiecki

Ilani Kopiecki, BA, CMT, Craniosacral Therapist, and owner of Ilani Sessions in Novato, Marin County CA, has been involved with the healing arts for over 25 years. She has been trained in many healing modalities, including Craniosacral Therapy for adults and pediatrics, intuitive body-work, and shamanic energy healing. Ilani holds an advanced certificate in Therapy from the Upledger Institute, a California State bodywork license, and has received extensive shamanic training from the Four Winds Institute. Ilani brings over 20 years of wisdom treating adults, infants, and children in her office and remotely. She has a life-partner of 39 years and a wonderful son. It is her joy to serve you and your loved ones.

Ilani invites you to visit her website at **ilanisessions.com**, or email her at **info@ilanisessions.com**.

GIVE YOURSELF A GREAT BIG HUG: PARTNER WITH YOUR BODY FOR OPTIMAL HEALTH
BY DEBORAH MYERS

Our world in 2020

As I write this in September 2020, the question that we hear the most is, "What are we going to have to deal with next?" As human beings, we are hard-wired with a "need to know." We are coping with so much—the pandemic and all the fallout, the underlying concern whether one's health is in jeopardy, and the violence that seems to be running rampant. All of that can create a lot of anxiety and stress because we don't know any outcomes. Additionally, depending on where you live, many are living with the threat of life-threatening storms, intense heat, or wildfires.

The anxiety from stress can take our breath away, wait with bated breath, and wait for the next shoe to drop. When that's the case, "held breath" can initiate other "projects" that can affect our physical, mental, and emotional well-being.

When we do our daily energy balancing, we help our bodies to not internalize the stress created from challenges. And, when our bodies don't take in and hold onto the stress, there is less likelihood that we'll end up with problems. Consequently, I suggest that my clients and students use the word "projects" instead of "problems." Projects have a beginning and an end, and they are a lot more fun to deal with than problems, no matter the type of challenge. Let's see what we can do to help YOU resolve those things called projects.

My entrance into the world of health care via my own project

In the spring of 2020, I celebrated my twenty-fifth year of being an alternative health care provider. It was in 1995 that I stepped into being an acupressurist and Jin Shin Jyutsu practitioner because it's the modality that helped me heal from my own project.

My physical and health challenges began on a day that seemed like any other day. I was driving through a residential neighborhood, looking forward to getting home after a long day. I put on my signal to change lanes and then—thwack!—my head hit the window. A moment later, there was another thud as my head was thrown against the window again.

Although it took three months before I understood the details of what had happened, the accident reverberated throughout my body loud and clear. I was in constant pain, I suffered horrible headaches, and my neck and back were seriously inflamed. No matter what my body was experiencing, I had to pay the bills. That meant I needed to continue working long hours in front of the computer, on the phone, and in the car driving to clients' homes. Not only was my body under severe stress, but my foggy mind made it close to impossible to keep up with the ever-growing must-do list.

What was incredibly hard was the fact that I didn't feel on top of it with my kids and their schedules—homework, school events, special programs, and sports. I was used to being "team mom" for my son's soccer team, and I volunteered in the classrooms several mornings a week. But so many of the activities I was used to doing, like rollerblading with the kids, were no longer options.

Despite the pain, I put on a stoic face and was able to take care of my work, home, and kids because, fortunately, for years, I had been studying and practicing self-help acupressure. By doing a daily routine to balance my energy system, I was able to function, but I knew I needed

an expert to help me fully heal. That's how I discovered Jin Shin Jyutsu, an ancient form of Japanese acupressure.

This gentle healing therapy strategically targeted critical acupressure points throughout my body, allowing it to release the inflammation and pattern of pain. I began to bend and move without difficulty. My clarity and focus improved, my productivity increased, and my outlook became brighter.

That's when the light bulb came on. After years of chasing down the right career, **I knew what I was meant to do. I closed my insurance and securities office and stepped into becoming an acupressurist and Jin Shin Jyutsu practitioner. Jin Shin Jyutsu had saved my body, mind, and spirit. I wanted to help others live more efficiently in their bodies too!**

That was 1995, and I cannot imagine turning back the clock to do it differently. I am truly living my passion, helping others live healthier, happier, and more productive lives. As I witness clients dramatically change how they live in their bodies, I cannot imagine a more rewarding profession. And that is especially the case with the world we are living in today.

Letting go of projects and challenges

I'm a believer that each of us can be our own care provider. We just need to be shown a technique that is easy to learn, easy to do, and easy to remember to do because it works. So why wouldn't we do something when the benefits are so noticeable?

One of my early clients was Sara, a thirty-five-year-old mother of young children, who lived with excruciating neck pain and debilitating headaches. As a result, she often missed work, and the quality of her life tanked. The doctors had diagnosed her with an "irreversible inflammatory disease," and told her the best she could hope for was to "contain the pain with medication."

Her situation was all too familiar, so I felt confident acupressure would help. As time progressed, Jin Shin Jyutsu allowed her more comfortable, flexible movement as her inflammation and pain decreased. Her emotions stabilized, and she reacted to daily stress and anxiety more calmly.

Now in her fifties, Sara enjoys a very full, active life. Thanks to the magic of Jin Shin Jyutsu, she resumed her nursing career. Today, her children, now in their twenties and thirties, look back on a happy childhood playing softball, backpacking, and biking with their mother.

While I was giving Sara one-on-one Jin Shin Jyutsu treatments, I also spent time teaching her self-help acupressure. The daily practice helped her stay ahead of the pain. Additionally, she applied what she learned to support her children. With her encouragement, as well as requests from many other clients, I created a series of workshops to teach self-help acupressure.

I wanted to show people how to be partners with their bodies. Non-intrusive and gentle, Jin Shin Jyutsu replenishes mental, physical, and emotional energy, and allows breathing to expand. Where energy flows, the breath follows. It seems like magic: it can reduce stress, balance emotions, improve performance, increase clarity and focus, and strengthen self-confidence and mindfulness. When we target pressure points to relieve bothersome symptoms and maintain energy balance, it's very empowering.

From the very beginning, I have taught all my clients a nine-step self-help acupressure routine that I call The Daily Clean Your House Flow®. As time went by, I wanted children to have an easy way to learn and experience energy balancing that was fun, so I created an animated video of the Daily Flow.

A third-grader convinced me to find ways to empower children to make a difference in their own lives. Joey told me that he was doing the Daily Flow several times a day because studying was easier, which resulted in his grades improving. He told me that he was even getting along better with his brother, saying, "That's crazy!" And then he said, "And I'm playing a better game of soccer. So, why wouldn't I do it?" It was noticeable to him that the Daily Flow was making a difference, so he decided to make it a part of his day.

Kristen was a highly motivated sixteen-year-old. She carried an intense load of classes, as well as pursued sports, music, and community service—all of which she felt were necessary to receive the scholarships she was hoping to obtain. But anxiety crept in, affecting her sleep, grades, sense of well-being, and emotional stability. Understandably, her parents were worried and sought out help. Receiving Jin Shin Jyutsu treatment and practicing self-help acupressure, allowed Kristen to break through the anxiety, fear, and worry. She graduated with honors, loves being at college, and now Kristen has tools she can rely on for the rest of her life. "Whenever I have feelings come up that I don't understand, I do my energy work, and I feel better," she says.

Stress affects the energetic balance of the body systems, as does trauma. In fall 2017, thousands of people in Sonoma County, California experienced trauma, beyond description, as they raced away from the blazing infernos that had been their homes. The impact from those few days of hell left emotional scars, particularly for youngsters.

I worked with Justin, a five-year-old who could not understand why he had lost his belongings, why he didn't have his old bedroom to go home to, and why his cat was no longer part of the family. He was suffering physical shortness of breath from smoke inhalation, plus his breath had been taken away by the trauma. The combination of physical and emotional manifestations caused him to be stuck in the memory and sadness he'd experienced, and recurring nightmares plagued him. As I applied gentle touch on energy meridian points, his lungs opened to release the buildup of smoke, his body remembered the old pattern of expansive breath, he broke through the nightmares, and he started smiling and laughing again. Justin and his parents learned how to do their own acupressure flows so he could consistently go to sleep and wake up rested and happy.

Why did the energy balancing of Jin Shin Jyutsu help Justin and his parents begin their healing and get their breath back after the fires? **It is energy that makes us tick! Each one of us is made up of energy, and it is supposed to flow and not be stuck. It's energy that helps all of our systems—immune, adrenal, endocrine, nervous, respiratory, digestive, vascular, muscular, skeletal—work individually and concurrently so our bodies can function smoothly.**

We can access that energy by placing fingertips on designated points to harmonize and restore the energy flow. Holding these points in combination, releases accumulated tension and resets the body to its natural state of balance. **Our bodies are miracles. When mind, body, and spirit are in balance, we can tap into the wisdom of the body, interpret the messages, and restore harmony. At that moment, the body is brought back to its full potential.**

Jin Shin Jyutsu helped Sara, Justin, Joey, and Kristen release tension and pain by balancing and replenishing mental, physical, and emotional energies. It transformed their lives, and it changed mine. **The best part is that this ancient acupressure is something we can do for ourselves. It empowers us with the understanding that health is at our fingertips, and it gives us the ability to take charge of our well-being.**

Self-Help Acupressure for you and your family members

First off, I recommend doing the Daily Clean Your House Flow®. It's a nine-step flow that creates a foundation of balance and harmony. Go to **www.deborahmyerswellness.com** and click on the purple button, "Learn the Daily Flow." You will get a copy of the Daily Flow as well as lots of energy tips for breath, clarity, and focus.

Check out the animated video of the Daily Clean Your House Flow® that kids are loving. Adults appreciate it just as much, since most of us are kids at heart.

As you have probably figured out, I'm a big believer in helping our bodies breathe, both with the expansion of the inhale and assisting the purging of the exhale. Now, more than ever before, we need to have ways to be in easy, effortless breath, to release anxiety, and to help our bodies feel healthy and vital. We need to stay ahead of the game and help our bodies be better prepared for what we ask them to do and better prepared for what might come at them.

Our kids especially need extra assistance amid distance learning. We want them to feel comfortable with learning, to enjoy a sense of belonging, and to experience success. And that's the case whether it's on-site or online. They can learn to be partners with their own bodies and have health at their fingertips.

The following suggestions work for all ages! Consider doing them for yourself and maybe create family gatherings so everyone can do them together.

When you're following these self-help steps, hold each pose with a light, gentle touch for at least several deep breaths. There's no such thing as too much self-help. So, do your energy balancing as often as you think of it!

For a strong, vital foundation that reduces stress, boosts your immune system, helps let go of old, chronic conditions, and balances emotions:

* Do the Daily Clean Your House Flow® at least once per day.
* Do the Jumper Cables as many times a day as you think of it.

Jumper Cabling (step 9 in the Daily Flow) is gently cupping each thumb and finger and holding each for several deep breaths. Help get rid of Worry FAST! (See the whole description on my website.)

* Consider a meditation practice. The Daily Flow can become part of that experience.

To connect with breath and create space for expansive inhales and purging exhales:

* Cross arms and hold fingers on upper arms.
* Right hand – hold fingers on base of right ribcage.
  Left hand – hold fingers on right chest below the collarbone.

* Switch hands to do the left side.
* Cup each thumb.

To create clarity and focus, improve performance and increase self-esteem and mindfulness:

1. Right hand – hold fingers on right base of skull.
   Left hand – hold fingers on left base of skull.
2. Right hand – cup back of head and hold left base of skull.
   Left hand – cup forehead with fingers on right forehead.
3. Left hand – cup back of head with fingers on right base of skull.
   Right hand – cup forehead with fingers on left forehead.

These simple clarity and focus tips have helped both kids and adults break through blocks that are in their way to moving forward, even pro-crastination! Additionally, they improve sleep patterns.

Invitation to Connect

I invite you to connect with me if you have any questions or ah-ha's as you step into your daily practice of balancing your energy.

Please consider sharing the information about my Productive Mindfulness School Program. It offers kids practical self-help tools that they can use any time. In less than 10 minutes a day, students can create a more positive, successful school experience, whether learning is happening at home or school. It's easy and fun, and it works!

Let's help our children learn how to move through stress!

Visit my website at **www.deborahmyerswellness.com** to check out my programs and workshops.

And for those who are interested in experiencing a session, please contact me at **deborah@deborahmyerswellness.com**. Or call me a (707) 546-5692. Sessions are offered in-person and virtual.

Wishing you effortless flow of balanced, calm, and healing energy!

Deborah Myers

A certified acupressurist, Jin Shin Jyutsu practitioner, author, speaker, and wellness coach, Deborah Myers helps people get and stay healthy. Since 1995, she has worked one-on-one with clients utilizing light, along with gentle touch to reduce stress and relieve pain, to bring balance to the body, mind, and spirit. Her sessions are available virtually, as well as in-person.

Deborah is on a mission to teach others how they can be partners with their own bodies. She founded Deborah Myers Wellness to treat, educate, inspire, and empower people of all ages to achieve balance and integrated health. She developed workshops, workplace wellness programs, and programs for kids in their classrooms and their homes. With the onset of Covid-19, all of the programs are now available virtually.

To share the magic of acupressure and Jin Shin Jyutsu with kids, Deborah created an animated video of the Daily Clean Your House Flow®, a nine-step self-help acupressure flow. She has written accompanying books that offer clear explanations and colorful illustrations.

Deborah developed the virtual Productive Mindfulness School Program to optimize learning and make life easier for everyone—kids, teachers, and parents. Her program, designed for K-8 students, empowers kids to step into an easy-to-do daily practice that will create calm, increase focus, balance emotions, and boost self-confidence, even during distance learning. The practical self-help tools help them succeed at home or school with resilience and grit.

Through her one-on-one Jin Shin Jyutsu treatments, coaching, workshops, workplace and school programs, and her "Easy Self-Help Acupressure" animated video and books, Deborah has helped thousands of people of all ages discover how they can take charge of their own health.

Deborah resides in Northern California, loves gardening and hiking, and loves to share how to better enjoy life!

www.deborahmyerswellness.com
deborah@deborahmyerswellness.com
(707) 546-5692
https://www.facebook.com/deborah.myers.7982
https://www.facebook.com/DeborahMyersWellness
https://www.linkedin.com/in/deborahmyerswellness/
https://www.youtube.com/channel/UCpGOAyUcZjjG_f9JWCz5aIw

TRANSFORM YOUR BODY MIND
WITH THE BENN METHOD™
BY LINDA BENN

You are an amazing soul that chose to be here at this incredible time on the planet to experience and witness what is happening, especially right now with a global pandemic underway. We are observing mass consciousness awakening. Remember who you are as a soul and how powerful you are. Keep your energy high, shine your light, and keep moving forward.

Advanced souls have karmically eventful lives. Many of us have experienced a traumatic past for our soul's evolution. On this journey, we have all agreed to go through these experiences for our soul's growth.

The Benn Method™ is a compilation of my 20 years as a practitioner. Plus, my learnings from hundreds of teachers, mentors, and coaches over the last 30-plus years who have assisted in healing from my past trauma, karma, and have helped me to understand what I agreed to learn in this lifetime.

The Benn Method™ is to help you go from trauma to thriving, resulting in freedom, love, peace, and joy. BENN = Balance, Energy, Nurture, and Nourish. The BENN Method™ assists you in returning to your true authentic self of empowerment from where you can heal your body and soul, leading to a place where you are free of suffering and at peace.

My method also incorporates the 5R Renewal program, a five-step process that includes the physical, emotional, mental, energetic, and spiritual, along with the five elements of earth, wood, fire, metal, and water. The purpose is to align your mind, body and spirit, to empower you to take charge of your health and wellbeing by self-healing your body.

The 5Rs stand for:

- Release
- Realign
- Restore
- Rebalance
- Re-energize

5R RENEWAL MODEL™

As a holistic practitioner, my focus on health and wellness is addressing the root cause of the problem not just the symptoms. This creates a space for deep healing work on the level of physical, emotional, and etheric bodies.

I was born in a small town on the east coast of Australia. Born into a family that didn't understand me as we vibrate at different frequencies. I have learnt to accept and love them for who they are. As a soul, I came in as this bright light of joy but knew I was different from others. I was born with a natural intuitive gift but I was trying to understand why my family didn't love or accept me. The more I shared my passions and purpose, the more I was ostracized. My life has been a journey to love and accept myself and not look outside for love or approval from others. My family are playing important roles and I forgive them.

Though in my past I was carrying so much emotional pain of being rejected, abandoned, and abused, I was constantly asking why am I here? Why did I choose this family? Why am I being judged, criticized, and abused? I didn't like being in this body or living this life, hence the eating disorder that started as a teenager when my sister kept telling me that I was fat, ugly, and many other descriptive words. I believed that in order to be loved by anyone, I had to be thin, otherwise I would never get a boyfriend! I had depression growing up with so much emotional pain and suffering, though on the outside I appeared happy in order to cover up the deep sorrow inside. I left home at 17 and moved to Brisbane for work. At 18, I received a letter from my mother telling me not to come home as I didn't have a home to come to. No one knew my story or the pain I was carrying. If anyone got too close to me, I would get scared to open my heart and be betrayed again. It was safer to shut down and run away and even leave the country. Hence, by age 30, I travelled all around the world to over 35 countries searching, wondering, where do I belong? Where is home and how do I love? Love was a painful word as I had never experienced it. I realized my true home is in my heart. It's not where I physically live or who loves me. I am loved and supported by spirit. It has taken years to heal my heart and love and accept myself. Everything I have experienced over the years was all for a purpose—to help others. I have been blessed with amazing teachers over the years and many masters guiding me on my healing path.

At 21, I met my first spiritual teacher when I had cancer. I was back-packing around the world for three years and I met him in San Jose, California. He helped me understand why I chose my family, what I was to learn, and my purpose for this life.

The turning point in my life was when I felt a calling to leave the corporate world and study natural medicine. This opened up a huge Pandora's Box, which I loved. I was a sponge absorbing as much as I could and continue to study. I started my holistic health business in 2000 in Australia focusing on healing the mind-body connection. This included intuitive bodywork, energy work, reiki, Pellowah healing, facial harmony balancing, cranial sacral, ortho-bionomy, NLP, hypnotherapy, time line therapy, coaching, trainer, assessor, and many other modalities. A big "aha" moment I received was that you cannot heal the physical body solely with the mind that created it—the two work together. This realization led me into teaching personal development workshops, coaching, and training to empower others to heal their own body. I channel profound messages for clients, as I know that we can change every cell in our body with our thoughts and by what we focus on.

In 2006, I travelled to the U.S. for a few months to teach Pellowah healing and share this powerful modality. Pellowah is a tool to help expand awareness and consciousness on the planet, which is in alignment with my purpose.

I relocated to live in California from 2010 to the end of 2016. I felt I needed to return to my home country to heal my relationship with my family for the next chapter of my life, though I was feeling exhausted, burnt-out, and lost. Living in another hemisphere was a safe distance. When I contacted my family, the attacks started again. I gave my power away and fell into a dark depression and created a disease.

I stopped using my healing tools and everything I knew logically. Even though I knew my soul's purpose, I gave up my will to live. I cut off my connection to source energy and disconnected from my inner child, resulting in my physical body quickly deteriorating. I was committing energetic suicide. I take total responsibility for creating disease in my body; it was my way of coping with past trauma. Even though my soul knew why I came here as a light worker, I had huge resistance and tried to end my contract several times as the emotional pain was so intense, though my masters guiding me kept intervening to stop that process.

I visited the dark side to experience where many people get stuck with depression, suicide, and illness. I had to go through it myself in order to relate and have compassion for others. I had everything stripped away so I could restructure my life.

You may have health-related issues, pain in your body, anxiety, or fatigue. Or you may want clarity to solve problems and transform anger, grief, shame, guilt, sadness, hurt, and childhood trauma. These experiences cause energy blockages and feeling out of balance, out of control, and having no direction in your life. I chose a healing career which helped me to heal and learn the skills to help others. I have experienced everything my clients come to me to resolve in their emotional past that was causing them disease. This led me to the formation of the 5R Renewal Program and Benn Method™.

We influence our genes by our thinking and consciousness and can manifest disease in our body, which I experienced. My body was in chronic stress causing an autoimmune disease, my thyroid TSH was 0.01, which is extremely low; now it is sitting at 3.0, which is normal.

Every organ and system was barely functioning. My liver was at 38%, my left eye was at 30%, I couldn't drive or focus. Now both eyes are great and I don't need glasses for long or short distances. This proves that we can heal every part of our body.

My brain could not concentrate or remember things. I was so fatigued, I had to keep having naps during the day. My adrenal test showed that I had phase three adrenal fatigue; it was a flat line on the graph. I had massive sleeping issues because my nervous system was constantly in stress response. Now I sleep soundly, have rebalanced my adrenals, and have my energy and mojo back.

I have been through my own recovery from cancer, chronic stress, adrenal burnout, chronic fatigue, autoimmune, suicide, depression, addictions and a 30-plus year eating disorder. Using my Benn Method and 5Rs, I naturally transformed and restored my body to full health without medication or any medical intervention.

There is a global problem of mental health, depression, suicide, eating disorders, feeling unlovable, unworthy, not good enough, self-judgement, self-criticism, addictions, and self-destructive behaviors. Many people are going through challenging times, feeling pushed to the limits, stressed, overwhelmed, anxious, frustrated, or simply unhappy.

Look at everything you do in your life: the activities, decisions you make, how you interact with others. All of this affects your energy vibration. Your words, thoughts, emotions, and beliefs create your reality. In my programs, I help you upgrade your conscious human operating system. Imagine your brain is a computer. Using my methods is like going from an old computer operating system like DOS, which is limited and full of viruses, to installing a new "heart ware" system, which is conscious, aware, and thriving.

By connecting to source and listening to your own internal GPS, you automatically upgrade your conscious human operating system. Your brain can make clear choices and decisions for your highest good and destiny. This is a time of enormous growth and opportunity spiritually, mentally, and emotionally. When you drop into your heart, you will feel an increase in YOUR love that will expand out and attract more. DO LOVE, BE LOVE, and be the example for others to follow and radiate your love and light. When you surrender, letting go of control and attachments, you allow yourself to receive more positivity, abundance, joy, peace, harmony, and happiness.

This is why I created the BENN method of four profound steps to help open your heart to feel love and light with every breath.

BENN stands for Balance, Energy, Nurture and Nourish = New Life.

BENN METHOD™

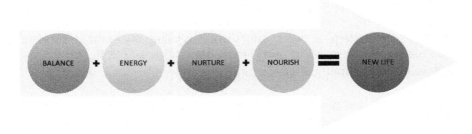

Balance all areas of your life – physically, emotionally, mentally, energetically, and spiritually. Listen to your body, your body is the barometer of the soul, guiding you to restore your health and wellbeing. When you ignore the body's signs or messages it can lead to disease. Any imbalance in your work or life can lead to adrenal burn out, sleep imbalances, and illness. My prior lifestyle was totally imbalanced, constantly pushing myself with work, over exercise, very little sleep, high cortisol, adrenal fatigue, and saying yes when I meant NO, which lead to my burnout.

When out of balance, you are in survival mode, which is a stress response of fight or flight. This drains your energy of vitality, health, and in the long-term leads to disease. To move back into balance is to learn to self-regulate by being present and just breathing. When you breathe deeply down to your belly, it sends a message to the rest of your body via your nervous system that you are safe in your environment. By simply breathing and connecting to your heart, this shifts you out of your mind, which created the illusion of stress, to a place of peace, harmony, and balance. When you're balanced, grounded, and focused, you attract more abundance, love, joy, and health into your life.

The meditation I teach calms your mind and body, allowing it to remain relaxed, balanced, peaceful, and harmonious. Your goal is to deflect the lower energies that throw you off balance and cause stress, feeling burdened, and suffering. When you drop your focus into your heart, it opens up to the joy of life.

Energy. You are a powerful energy being connected to source energy. You can shift the energy, heal your body, and change the cells in your body by your intention and thought. Life force energy is flowing through you constantly. This allows you to remain high vibration, energetic, and live a joyful life with vitality. When I cut off my connection from source, my energy and physical body quickly deteriorated. This is why it's so important to connect to source through meditation, breathing, and feeling the flow of energy to heal your body. Now's the time to deepen your connection with source and upgrade your heart-ware, and to co-create everything you desire in your life. Sleep is vital for your energy to make clear choices throughout the day.

Nurture is all about self-love, self-acceptance, self-worth, self-awareness, self-care, self-compassion, self-forgiveness, nurturing your inner child, and listening to your soul's calling. Look at your shadow-self that requires healing and nurturing. Do you see your body through the eyes of love? This was a big learning moment for me when navigating out of an eating disorder. Give to yourself first, through selfcare. Fill up your cup, be kind and loving to you! This can simply be by taking a bath, saying NO to others, taking a nap, or sitting quietly in a garden and having a cup of tea. When you tune into your heart, you can transform any reaction into a loving action which improves your overall health and wellbeing.

Nourish your mind and body. Make healthy food choices for your body. Read books to feed your mind and consciousness. Nourish your soul with meditation and healing techniques, personal development tools, allow yourself to surrender and let go to what is. Always come back to the present moment and breathe. Fill yourself up with source energy. Focus on thoughts, people, and activities that make you feel good and nourish your soul.

To support you on your journey to vibrant health, I encourage you to commit to a 33-day habit to rewire your brain to accelerate results in your life.

Repeat this mantra to say, "All my needs are met for my physical, emotional and spiritual body." I surrender, I release, I let go . . .

With this mantra, you will begin to experience more of what you desire, while peace and gratitude will flow freely into your space. By embracing that gratitude, you welcome more powerful energy to help create your desires.

YOU are here to vibrate your light—let it shine!

Life is about freedom. We are all here to experience the freedom and love within us.

Mantra to repeat through the day—I feel so blessed to be alive today.

I would love to support you on this journey called life. Please feel free to contact me at **linda@lindabenn.com**, and make sure to tap into the following gifts on my site: meditation, consultation, and the 33-Day Challenge Guide. Go to **www.lindabenn.com/rewireyourbrain**

Linda Joy Benn

Linda Joy Benn, MT. Msc is an international professional speaker, coach, and practitioner specializing in holistic health. Her mission is to help professional women thrive by empowering them to lead a healthier, happier, and more productive life. Having overcome cancer, chronic fatigue, autoimmune, suicide, depression and an eating disorder without medical intervention, Linda has the expertise and knowledge to support people during their struggles with illnesses and trauma-related issues.

Linda is the founder of the BENN Method™ (BENN= Balance, Energy, Nurture & Nourish). It's a sustainable method that empowers professional women to let go of stress and trauma as they become healthier and happier, resulting in a new passion for life. She travels between Australia and the USA to share her passion and enthusiasm for helping to transform others to heal their body and soul, reduce suffering from emotional and physical pain, and be at peace within themselves.

Over the last 20 years, Linda has transformed thousands of people's minds and bodies through her holistic approach. As a medical intuitive, Linda quickly identifies the root cause of blocked energy in order to shift it in the body and mind, bringing the life-force energy to that area, which results in miraculous healing and transformation.

- As well as helping individuals, Linda has created the 5R Renewal program. The program is the foundation for the BENN Method: Release, Realign, Restore, Rebalance and Reenergize. It's a 5-step process that includes the physical, emotional, mental, energetic, and spiritual aspects. Suitable for business owners and employees alike to become more effective, engaged, and enthusiastic about their job.

Linda's wisdom and teachings are a strong foundation for healing skills, intuitive wisdom, self-empowerment, creativity, clarity, and for igniting one's uniqueness, purpose, and unlimited potential.

linda@lindabenn.com
+61-412 586 528
www.lindabenn.com
https://www.facebook.com/lindajoybenn
https://www.facebook.com/lindabenninternational
https://www.facebook.com/groups/VitalitywithLinda
https://www.linkedin.com/in/lindabenn/
https://www.youtube.com/channel/
UCBN5gmikYLp38VCcMRUDqsw

PART TWO: FOCUSED INTENTION

MOVING TOWARD MASTERY

A DIFFERENT LOOK AT SELF-CARE
BY CATERINA RANDO

When conversations happen around self-care, the discussion often covers more sleep, exercise, improved nutrition, increased hydration, and the like. All of these things and others like them relate to our physical self-care and are very important. In this chapter, however, I will focus on emotional and mental self-care. How we behave with others, the decisions we make or do not make, what we choose to do or not do, can also significantly impact our self-care.

I have had my own business for many years and one of the great things about self-employment is that it challenges you to develop skills that allow you to take care of your business at the same time you are developing the ability to take better care of yourself. Having been raised by a gracious school teacher, an academic engineer, and nuns at the Catholic schools I attended, I would say that when I started my own business in my late 20s, I was not very skilled at asking for what I wanted or articulating what did not work for me. These are skills I was taught in a seminar somewhere and fortunately, being a young woman on a mission, my business gave me a lot of chances to learn those skills. These are two important skills I hope you have developed as they are key to your outstanding self-care. Following in this chapter are a few more skills I would like to share with you. You will get to see if you could use an upgrade so that your self-care encompasses your communication, your decisions, and the actions that are right for you.

Get More Support by Asking for It

Recently, after an event, I gave someone a ride back to their hotel even though it was in the opposite direction I was going. I was happy to do it and it got me thinking, what adds ease more than anything else?

What happens when we ask for help? For instance, asking someone for a ride or a review or a resource or a referral? We usually get what we have asked for — easily. Not only do we get what we want, we are also giving someone else an opportunity to help us, to give to us, to be of service.

When others give to us, they get something in return. First, they feel a personal satisfaction from helping, this makes them feel better about themselves. In addition, they get our gratitude and appreciation. This can be expressed privately in words, or through a phone call or a note. We can also thank them publicly on our Facebook page, in our ezine, or from the front of the room at an event.

Asking others for help will help you remember that you do not have to do everything yourself. In fact, you will feel less stressed or overwhelmed when you get some support. Start asking yourself what can you use help with: a handyman to fix that chair, a gardener to keep up with it all, a cleaning lady just because you hate cleaning. Self-care is very much about freeing up our time to do what we care to do and not what we think we should do or what has to be done that we do not want to do. Honor yourself by asking for support in all areas of your life. Take a moment right now and reflect on the different areas of your life: your home, your car, your closets, your work, your kids, your health, your relationships, your finances, your get away plans, your spiritual life or your emotional life. Is there anywhere in these areas or any others that you can use some support? Support is not being indulgent, it is not spoiling yourself—it is self-care. Go get more support today.

Choose to Be More Decisive

When I take women on retreats, one of the activities we do is a jewelry exchange. Everyone brings jewelry or accessory items they are no longer interested in but they think someone else would really enjoy. Then we quickly pass the items around, each woman has to make an insta-decision if she wants an item that is passed to her or if she wants to pass it on. While we have fun, it is also an exercise in making decisions quickly. Note that decision-making is an important self-care skill because too often women oscillate for minutes, hours, days, weeks, even I have spent a month pondering, contemplating, researching, discussing a decision from all possible angles before making a decision. Many times, we don't realize that indecisiveness keeps us struggling. Nothing can move forward, no action can be taken until a decision is made. Time is being wasted, experience is not being gained, revenue is not being generated when no conclusion for the right course of action had been finalized.

I remember a time when I woke up every morning saying to myself that I did not want to be in a relationship with my partner anymore. This was after months of vacillating back and forth about what to do about my relationship. After five days of waking up with these thoughts I made the decision to break off the relationship. Yes, it was scary, yes there were many things that would need to be figured out, yes there would be my partner's upset to deal with and many uncomfortable moments to endure, and yet, once the decision was made, everything started to move toward resolution. That was some time ago, a new better and more fulfilling life chapter unfolded only after the decision was made. Is there a place in your life where you have been putting off a decision because it will not be easy after that decision is made? Is there a place in your life where you feel stuck? Maybe that is because you have been putting off a decision.

Create Criteria to Make Decisions Easier

This section here will support you in getting better at your decision making. Making decisions is self-care because decisions bring clarity, which relieves worry and stress, and facilitates us being true to ourselves. Often times, women have difficulties making decisions because we have not created criteria for different aspects of our lives. For example, I encourage you to create criteria for who gets to be your friend. Any friend of mine has to be kind, have a good heart and nature, have integrity, be reliable, and be a genuine caring person. When I meet a person who wants to be social and get to know me and it becomes clear they do not meet these criteria, then it is easy for me to let the relationship go. The interesting thing is that when you create criteria you will quickly begin to notice when someone does not meet it. If you do not have one, then you will notice that something is off, you will often not be quite sure what it is because you have not taken the time to decide what is okay and what is not okay for you.

Where in your life can you use criteria? Create one for your significant relationship and create one for anyone you hire. My gardener, my handyman, and my housecleaner all meet a criteria of being professional, kind, reliable, honest, and good at communicating. This might seem obvious to you, however, often times as women we accommodate behaviors that don't work for us. We perhaps even unconsciously want to be liked more than we want to do what works for us, and so we allow ourselves to be taken advantage of because we have not taken the time to determine in advance what is acceptable or not acceptable to us. Is there a place in your life where you set criteria?

Manage Your Disappointment and Uplift Your Life

A while back I gave a speech to a group of women entrepreneurs, my ideal clients. At the end of my speech, I invited the ladies to attend my upcoming event at a deep discount. Only one person in an audience of 60 women signed up for the event. When I went home, I was very disappointed, I felt like I had wasted all that time preparing, I even felt a little sad and depressed. Then within five days, seven ladies of the ladies in that audience had taken me up on my offer.

That was the day I decided to never again be disappointed by the immediate results I see in business or in life. How something appears right now is not necessarily the final result for how it will be. When we forget this truth we often take ourselves on an emotional rollercoaster of disappointment, second-guessing ourselves and doubting our abilities. When you are not satisfied with a situation or current result, or feel you are not getting enough back for the energy you are expending, if you are like most people, this will likely result in being less productive, unfocused, and not acting. Cut all this out.

Recognize that your perspective is paramount to your effectiveness in all aspects of life. When something does not go as you had hoped, instead of telling yourself you might have made the wrong decision, ask yourself what you can do to make your decision right. Sometimes you can turn around a situation that does not initially go your way. The thing to remember here is that disappointment does not serve you. Notice it and realize that things change and let it go, allowing yourself to move on.

Look for the learning. Every time things do not go as well as planned we have an opportunity to evaluate what we could have done better. We can make upgrades and then reap more rewards next time. "Always be upgrading" is a great guiding principle for all aspects of your life. Is there a place in your life where you have a lot of disappointment? Is there something you can do to add an upgrade?

Master Your Self-Talk

The other important thing to focus on in terms of communication as it relates to self-care is how we communicate with ourselves. Everything you say to yourself either serves you or sabotages you, you get to choose. Which side are you on? I want to be very clear, you get to choose. You have messages about who you are that were imbedded in your ears, perhaps decades ago. Someone said you were shy, and maybe you were at seven, but that does not mean you are still shy at 47. You still believe it is true because you have not examined that idea in decades.

I invite you to consider what kind of person you want to be and to become more aware of the thinking and messages you give to yourself. Do you want to be a positive person? If so, then talk as positively to yourself as you do to others.

What we say to ourselves matters because we are listening. Start to speak well of yourself to yourself. Notice old messages that do not serve you and eliminate them, replace them with new thoughts about who you are or are seeking to be. Tell yourself people look forward to being with you, that you are the kind of person that inspires others, and someone people want to be around. The more you focus on the positive side of who you want to be, not only will you uplift yourself, you will also begin to shift your self-perception from who you are to who you want to be. What are some messages for you to disregard and what are some messages that serve you that you should embrace? Make a list and start supporting yourself more with your self-talk.

We have explored some different ideas about self-care in this chapter around your decision making, using your voice to gain support, managing your disappointment, and mastering your self-talk. Pick an area above that you are going to focus on and improve. After all, self-care means taking care of all aspects of who you are. Shine the spotlight on what we have discussed here and uplift your self-care and your life. You deserve a life filled with bliss.

Caterina Rando

Caterina Rando serves women on a mission to serve and massively monetize their mastery. She shows entrepreneurs how to be loud and proud about the value they bring in order to make their businesses thrive. Her clients grow, shine, expand, open themselves up to new possibilities, and take their businesses further than ever before. Caterina is all about, positivity, integrity, generosity, community, and providing massive value while uplifting others.

She is a sought after speaker, event producer, and author. Her latest book is the ABCs of Public Speaking. Her book, Learn to Think Differently, from Watkins Publishing is published in over thirteen countries and several languages.

Caterina wants women to know that they do not have to wait until they are wealthy or retired before they can embrace philanthropy. She is the co-author of the Women's Giving Circle Guide.

Caterina is also the founder of the Thriving Women in Business Center, located in San Francisco. This is an attractive and warm place for women to come and do their workshops. Caterina's plan is to open more centers throughout Northern California.

Caterina is recognized for her special way of infusing business with making a difference. She has received the Extraordinary Woman Award from Developing Alliances. The American Businesswomen Association bestowed on her the Woman of Distinction Award and she has also received the Limitless Woman Award from the Limitless Woman Conference.

Caterina is the founder of the Thriving Women in Business Community, made up of all the women in her advanced programs and some program graduates.

She holds a Bachelor of Science in Organizational Behavior and a Master of Arts in Life Transitions Counseling Psychology. She is a Certified Personal and Professional Coach (CPPC) and a Master Certified Coach (MCC), the highest designation awarded by the International Coaching Federation.

Email Address: **cat@caterinarando.com**
Phone Number: 415-350-6854
Website: **caterinarando.com**
Facebook page(s): **www.facebook.com/thrivingbusiness**
LinkedIn Page: **www.linkedin.com/in/caterinarando**
Twitter handle : @caterinarando
YouTube Channel: **www.youtube.com/user/CaterinaRando/featured**
Instagram: **www.instagram.com/caterina_rando**

OWNING YOUR SELF-WORTH
BY WENDY LEE BALDWIN HARGETT

When was the last time that you honestly felt really great about your-self on the deepest level? Gave yourself a compliment as you gazed into your reflection in the mirror or store front window? How long does the smile on your lips last before it fades and twists into a frown or scowl? How long before the sneering, scornful voice of your inner critic snaps you back into "reality?"

What do you hear inside yourself when someone comments on how nice you look today or how mouth-watering the delicious three-course meal is that you spent tireless energy creating? Do you deflect these compliments by shrugging them off, shrinking up inside, or feel the heat on your cheeks as you blush? Insisting that, no, you don't look pretty or the meal was "nothing" and will taste better next time?

If you're like many people, you've never truly held your head high, shoulders square, and walked with confidence. You've never owned without a doubt in your heart and soul, that you are amazing. Or if you did, perhaps it was a fleeting moment that dashed with the wind, rarely repeated.

Do you live to please others, even if doing so, means that you paint on another fake smile because their happiness is more important than yours?

How are your relationships? Are you treated with love and respect at all times? Do you struggle making ends meet financially?

If any of this sounds like you, then you are silently suffering with your self-worth and may not even realize it.

That's how my life used to be.

My birth father resented the concept of my existence and beat my mother as if she was a naughty child while she was pregnant with me. My fetal-self absorbed the energy of my rage filled father like a sponge. His message left me knowing that, without a doubt, I wasn't worth giving birth to. Since emerging out of the womb, feeling like God's biggest mistake, a black cloud buried itself in my heart and soul, apologizing every day for being alive and taking up space that should have been for someone else.

At the insistence of my father, my birth parents gave me up for adoption as an infant. My new mother grew weary and resentful from the burden of tending to a child that wasn't hers by birth. Changing my diapers and comforting my cries quickly grew old and tiresome. Often abandoning me in my crib, while she consorted with her secret lover. She was out of my life before I turned two.

My new dad did the best he could to take care of me, but as a single father, the heavy responsibility of juggling work and tending to an active child was a circus juggling act at times. He married my stepmother just after my seventh birthday. The honeymoon quickly ended for all of us. It didn't take long to understand that I was still a burden. Worthless. A bother. My heart and voice didn't matter. In hopes of tempering down the onslaught of nagging and whining from his wife, Dad opted to send me away to live in a religious cult community. The one-way ticket out of state screamed volumes that my ten-year-old self couldn't fully decode beyond I was worthless and unwanted.

My stint away from home lasted ten painful months. Feeling unsure and timid about my welcome home, I crossed the threshold of my old house and stepped into the unknown. Unfortunately, the newness of my return quickly faded. My stepmother and I slid right back into our groove of her resenting my existence and me stuffing my sadness, knowing that

I wasn't good enough, regardless of how hard I tried to be a good girl. One can't help but wonder if perhaps my coming home was a mistake too. Because before I knew it, the hostility and abuse were even worse than before. If only I could curl up and disappear.

One of my many secrets that I held deep inside for decades is that while living at the commune, I took myself out into the woods. My plan was to wander around aimlessly, deeper and deeper into the trees with the intent of getting lost, never be found, and die. At the time, I felt dejected that instead of getting lost, I ended up walking in circles, angry at God for not granting my wish.

At the age of eight, my dad sat me down on his bed and showed me pictures of my two older siblings and explained why I was with him instead of them. The black and white photos of my older sister and brother piqued lots of questions from my curious mind. The concept of adoption was a bit confusing so I asked Dad how much he paid for me. His response that he didn't pay anything drilled even further into my psyche that I was worthless, not even worth paying for. Even at that impressionable age, I knew that you had to pay for something you valued.

What I didn't realize until I hit my fifties is that I was a gift. Not an object to be purchased.

To cope with the onslaught of tension, abuse, belittlement, and shame, I stuffed my emotions deep in the pits of my gut and soul. As a teen, I started numbing myself with my new friends who never judged me, thought I was funny, cute and pretty dang cool— alcohol and junk food.

Even though I'd find myself surrounded by family and friends, my heart ached from loneliness and I beat myself up over a never-ending list of alleged misdeeds and insecurities.

By the time I hit my forties I was an emotional and physical mess and in dire need of help before totally falling apart. For as long as I can remember, I battled between wanting to live and the solace of death. Killing myself felt like an easy way to end the pain. I was worthless anyway and believed that I wouldn't be missed.

It's tragic how many of us grow up struggling with our self-worth, devaluing ourselves, or feeling insignificant. Dare I say, it's a problem of pandemic proportions. The more people I encounter, the more this gross misunderstanding of one's worthiness exposes itself and comes out of hiding. This is a good sign. Because as the saying goes, "You cannot change what you don't acknowledge."

How did we get this way and how do we overcome it and feel good about ourselves?

You were a vulnerable, impressionable, innocent child once too. What happened in your past that lead you to believe that you were anything less than perfection?

Perhaps something as seemingly harmless and positive as your mother made you share your favorite toy with your annoying younger sibling and you didn't want to. Or you were scolded for something, that as an adult doesn't seem like a big deal, but as an innocent child, it devastated you and knocked away a piece of your confidence and self-worth.

As a child, you experienced life through many filters, and self-worth is one of those. Then you carried the cross into adulthood. And life, in all of its challenges, reinforced subconscious beliefs about yourself.

Whatever happened to you, big or small, I'm sorry for your pain.

Know this: there is hope. You don't have to live the rest of your life feeling timid or undeserving. Now is the time to start allowing yourself to glow from the inside out when someone compliments you.

You can claim your right to wear a genuine smile right now. You can stand self-assured that you deserve the best that life has to offer. The best relationships, plenty of money in your bank account, and vibrant health.

You never did anything wrong. You simply didn't understand the bigger picture of life and your surroundings at the time. You were a vulnerable child in a confusing grown-up world run by adults who were confused, little kids on the inside who felt scared and unworthy too.

Science and psychology show that a child's brain is like a sponge and they are unable to filter out reality from fantasy like an adult can. That's why they believe in the Easter Bunny and Tooth Fairy. Children take in what is spoken and unspoken and then form beliefs around the energy and perceptions of events, other people's moods, and environment, then make it their truth.

What's tricky about the constrictive emotions that we lug around inside us, is that we get good at tampering them down for a little while, perhaps years or decades, or five minutes. Then something, or nothing happens and BAM! There's that self-defeating voice again, blaring inside your head and whole being, reminding you that you could have done something better, you're never going to be pretty enough, or smart enough . . .

Lack of self-worth often leads to some sort of rejection of ourselves, or others. We can play a bit of tug-of-war in relationships. Perhaps a bit passive aggressive.

Push people away, then wonder why, then get angry that we're all alone, feeling sorry for ourselves.

Where do your worthiness challenges silently rule your world, unknowingly robbing you of your joy and expansion?

Do you notice this in your relationships that are rocky or unfulfilling? Do you always have enough money? What about your job and co-workers? How is your health?

Some people express their lack of self-worth by being meek, mild, and eager to please. Others unleash their pain through rage, lashing out at others, and with an over inflated sense of self. A narcissist. Both ways host sad and wounded little kids inside, longing to feel loved and that they matter. That they are worthy.

Here's something else you may find fascinating: your feelings of unworthiness might not even be yours. What I mean by that is, as a child who absorbed everything, there is a good chance that you took on your parents' beliefs about their worthiness. Research proves that you inherit emotions and beliefs from your parents at conception as well as generational influences. If your belief system supports it, past lives can play a role too. I see this often in my clients. A powerful question to ask yourself is, "Is this my belief or someone else's?"

From a metaphysical perspective, what the experts have discovered is that your body can turn stored constrictive emotions like anger, sadness, fear, hurt, guilt, shame, rejection, and unworthiness into disease, affecting your organs, cells, skin, how old or youthful you look, and your brain function. *They found that your feelings of being unworthy and low self-esteem are often stored in your spleen, pancreas, or sex organs.

You can develop digestive issues, adrenal fatigue, weight challenges, lack of energy, or motivation, and even cancer, just to name a few.

My body manifested anxiety, depression, serious digestive issues, thyroid issues, adrenal fatigue and more. Doctors threw their hands up, unable to help me.

What I did was turn to holistic healing. Investing heavily in myself because on some level, a tiny part of me must have hoped that I was worth it. Because of what I went through, not only did I learn to heal myself, find my self-worth and claim my rightful place on earth, I also took the path of helping others do the same. I've been on a mission for over a dozen years, becoming an expert in the holistic and personal growth field. This means I've invested heavily in my own personal growth as well being a constant student and highly certified master practitioner, holistic healer, coach, author, and speaker. I'm known for holding sacred, loving space for people like you to heal and claim your worthiness.

Here are three ways you can practice self-care and start owning your self-worth today. (These steps are simple, yet powerful. It's okay if you struggle at first. That's normal. The key is to believe in yourself and never give up.)

1.) Sit in silence with your eyes closed, get in touch with your heart, and ask for an image of your younger self to come forward. Have a conversation as if that part of you is actually right in front of you. Lovingly tell your younger self that he/she is amazing, brave and beautiful. You can even hug and embrace your younger self. Send lots of love and say "I love you" out loud. Express the tender words of adoration and encouragement that you wanted and needed to hear at that age.

Give your younger self a voice. Let yourself have imaginary conversations, spoken through you, and express all the feelings and words that you couldn't because it wasn't safe, or there wasn't anyone to listen.

Know this: your source, whether it's God, Spirit, Universe, didn't create a mistake or someone less than worthy. That's a belief that you unwittingly took on as a kid and carried forward into the now.

2) Look at yourself in the mirror, even if it feels uncomfortable. Notice the texture of your hair and how it is combed, the shape of your nose, and color of your eyes. Look at how your lips curve as you smile or frown.

Say out loud, "*I love you, I'm proud of myself for* _____. *I am beautiful and worthy.*"

Notice what happens inside your body. What does your heart do? How does this *feel*? If you find yourself hesitating or avoiding yourself in the mirror, it's okay. Acknowledge how you feel and then do it for at least a moment anyway. With time and practice, this will get easier.

3) Watch and be mindful of your language and what you say about yourself. Your I Am is the strongest description of yourself. Your inner-child is listening. Your cells are listening. Your whole body is listening. You wouldn't tear down an innocent child or your best friend, right? Speak kindly, positively, and powerfully about and to yourself, because remember you're listening.

I'd love to hear how these steps help you. Reach out and let me know! Also, if you're ready to expand and own your worthiness faster, deep into your soul, let me know. We can set a time to connect. To get started right now, you can scan the QR code provided and have instant access to a gift from me to you that will help you with your worthiness.

It's important that you remember this:

You are priceless! You deserve the best. You deserve peace, love, joy, and unlimited abundance.

Know that you are beautiful, inside and out. Own the truth that you are a gift too. You are worthy and priceless!

Most importantly, always remember that you are loved and that you matter.

*Sources: Dr. Bradly Nelson, Dr. Randall Robirds and Dr. Alex Holub

Wendy Lee Baldwin

Wendy Lee Baldwin Hargett is a certified Master Success Coach, Master NLP Practitioner, Master Hypnotherapist, Spiritual Coach, and holistic healer. She is also a speaker and author of *Healing Your Soul in A Chaotic World: Defying The Odds of Sanity and Survival,* an unconventional blueprint for letting go and transforming your life. Wendy is known for helping people de-stress, turn their pain story into their love story to have better relationships, emotional well-being, and connection to Source. Through her fun and playful energy, Wendy helps clients feel safe, which decreases the "scary" part of change.

She provides a safe place for those to turn to who feel broken, alone, and in dire need of love, transformation, acceptance, and discovering their true I AM.

Wendy also helps entrepreneurs discover their missing link to ultimate success in business and personal life. The Haute Entrepreneur a.k.a., The Haute E.

Website: **https://www.alignwithjoy.com**
Email: **info@alignwithjoy.com**
Phone: 808-268-2407
Facebook group: **www.facebook.com/groups/thealignwithjoycircle/**
Instagram: @wendyleebaldwinhargett
YouTube: Wendy Lee Baldwin Hargett - The Haute Entrepreneur
QR code link: **https://www.alignwithjoy.com/pl/211422**

EMBRACE YOUR "INNER FAMILY" TO HEAL OLD WOUNDS AND UNLEASH YOUR TRUE SELF
BY DR. BETH HALBERT

Many years ago, I participated in a workshop focused on helping people tell their stories. One of the exercises in the workshop was to write your story, detailing the good, the bad, and the ugly about your life—the people and places that influenced you, and the beliefs and biases you held. If that wasn't hard enough, the next step certainly was. We had to read our stories out loud to a partner over and over again.

The room hummed as people read their life stories to one another. After a time, laughter started rippling across the room. People started seeing the absurd and obvious as they repeatedly read their stories to their partners.

At midnight, there were three people still holding on to the significance of their stories. I was one of those three. I was so attached to my story that I couldn't see straight. After all, it was my life! It was the story I had been telling myself and others for years. I held on to it like a dog to a bone. I had to choose to "fake laugh" and be inauthentic, or go home with my "significant" story and my tail between my legs. I chose the latter and created this process to heal the rest of my life!

By the next day, it was over! I stayed up all night creating the most powerful story tool that I still use today. *I finally got it!* I saw the perfection and humor of my story and how it had served me all those years. **I learned that while many people, events and actions *influenced* my life story, I *was no longer a* VICTIM *of my circumstances.***

Talk about an eye-opener! Who knew that I could consciously choose what EVERYTHING in my life meant to me! I could create stories that brought me pain and suffering, or I could create ones that brought me absolute JOY and my IDEAL OUTCOMES. **This realization changed my life forever and has compelled me to share it with you now.**

I finally understood that I had the power to consciously create and live into any story that I chose to believe. If I didn't like something in my life, I could change the story and live that new story and manifest my ideal outcomes. And I have!

This chapter chronicles a tiny part of my own personal story, a part of the tool I wrote that night (over 20 years ago). It provides a full overview of the "inner family" members that shape our daily lives, and offers ways for you to learn how to create your new story/stories.

I created this journey to help you identify the stories you hold near and dear to your heart that may no longer be serving you as an adult. The questions I have for you are, "Who is telling you these stories, what is the emotional age of the storyteller, and how are those stories working for you?" At the end of the chapter, I'll ask if you want to hold on to these stories or if you want help utilizing the full tool I created that night so you can live into the conscious life of your dreams. (By the way, what age is your dreamer? And are you still dreaming?)

What's Your Story and How Is It Working for You?

Here's the first step:

Write your story about a specific aspect of your life (e.g. parenting, health, money, relationships, work, sexuality, etc.).

Read it over and over to yourself.

Read it out loud so you become more objective about the story. (Recording it while reading aloud can help facilitate the process.)

If you are still unable to change your story, share your story and your ongoing thinking process with someone you are close to and trust.

If you are like me and this part didn't "fix" you, then you may want to take it to the next level. To help you get the most out of this process, it will be useful to meet your inner family (your unconscious thoughts, your blind spots, and the young aspects that may be ruling your life).

Your Inner Family

Many, if not all, of our stories have been created by these young emotional parts and developmental aspects of ourselves. By understanding how these stories have served these young parts and finding new and improved ways to meet their needs internally, your stories will no longer sabotage your life and what you want to consciously create.

This is your inner family: your inner three-year-old, your inner seven-year-old, your inner teen and your divine wise self. (When you understand each of these parts, you will learn how to integrate your internal conflicts and compassionately fall in love with ALL of you!)

Our inner family can be thought of as the emotional foundation of our authentic selves. Self-recognition, self-awareness, healing, and growth all stem from the development of our inner family.

The inner family consists of:

a very young self, your vulnerable inner three-year-old—I call mine "little b."

a young child self, your perfectionistic inner seven-year-old—I call mine "super b."

a teenage self, your bodacious, outrageous inner teen—I call mine "bubblin' b."

a wise adult self, your all-loving divine wise self—I call mine "Dr. B."

Later, I will explain how you can expand upon the traditional wounded inner child concept to include the inner seven-year-old and the inner teen. Adding the inner seven-year-old self and the inner teen self allows you to encompass not only the vulnerable and formative years of development, but also the spiritual, moral, mental, physical, sexual, and self-expressive aspects of development.

The FUN journey we will be sharing together is not about whether you were loved or whether you developed properly emotionally as a child. Instead, your inner family represents a series of emotional growth stages we *all* experienced and continue to experience during our lifetimes. As you begin to recognize the difference between your inner three-year-old, your inner seven-year-old and your inner teen, she/he will give voice to all the emotions, beliefs and stories you are experiencing and/or have held onto throughout your life.

Your Inner Family Characteristics

To get a copy of your inner family chart with all their characteristics, needs, desires, triggers, and other aspects, go to **www.DrBeth.com/ FreeStuff**.

The inner three-year-old

The emotional, scared, vulnerable, raw child within us is our inner three-year-old. This part of us is creative and energetic and has a zest for life. She/he dreams big, desires, wishes, has fantasies, and is joyful. A wounded inner three-year-old—who is often hidden, protected, and "taken care of" by our inner seven-year-old—can be sad, mad, upset, internally focused, sees oneself as a victim, is needy, dependent, irresponsible, needs much attention, is consumed by drama, is self-doubting, feels lack, fears with intense feelings, is creative, and can be "full of it" (spit and vinegar, spunk and life). She/he can also be carefree, playful, passionate, creative, full of life. The inner three-year-old has a close connection to your inner spirit self (i.e. magical manifester and powerful thinker). Sometimes it's hard to find, see, or feel the inner three-year-old because she/he is protected so well by our inner seven-year-old.

The inner seven-year-old

The inner seven-year-old is the moralist, parent-like, super hero, do-gooder, critic, know-it-all, hard worker, and people pleaser. This "feels-really-grown-up" child can be externally focused, over responsible, needs success, quite defensive, perfectionistic, and can feel overwhelmed with life. She/he is always right and usually judgmental. The inner seven-year-old is parent-like, parading around like an adult. She/he can also be organized, practical, considerate of others, seeing how the pieces fit together. The inner seven-year-old is the one trying to get everything done and, as the rule maker and rule follower, works hard to keep every-one safe from risk and playing "too big."

My theory is that most of the time, the vast majority of adults live and work as the structured, organized, rule-following, workaholic, perfec-tionistic inner seven-year-old. A large percentage of these hard-work-ing inner seven-year-olds are actually emotional inner three-year-olds pretending to be an all-grown-up inner seven-year-old. You can spot an inner three-year-old by the emotional outrage and exaggerated defen-siveness. Look carefully to find the scared, vulnerable, hurt, sad little inner three-year-old hiding behind the emotional tirade. You might even feel as if you are being attacked by a self-righteous, entitled teenager in a full-grown adult body.

The inner teen

The inner teen is the rule breaker, the risk taker, the exhibitionist who has the "teenager" attitude. She/he is an idealist and a pessimist simulta-neously, making absolutely no logical rational sense to our inner seven-year-old. She/he self-judges harshly while aspiring to be the superstar, the football hero, the runway model. The inner teen can't stand the mirror of anything "wrong" within themselves that they see in others. She/he has a self-conscious body image and/or an over-inflated body image, is irre-sponsible (yet expects to have it all given to them on a silver platter), has intense peer needs (yet wants freedom from all responsibility), is passion-ate and sexual, lives for full self-expression, is creative and open to new experiences, craves independence with no cost or accountability, blames others, and ignores or defies society's moral code. Just as our inner seven-year-old protects our inner three-year-old self, the inner teen protects us from our perfectionistic, workaholic inner seven-year-old. The inner teen is trying to protect our souls and trying to protect our passion and fun.

Part of the inner teen is the inner seven-year-old pretending to be a "cool teen." You can spot them by their moralistic, self-righteous indignation with a colorful judgmental flair. Look hard at the happy-go-lucky attitude and at the worry-and-plan-of-attack for whatever may go wrong. You may see the worried, anxious inner seven-year-old—who is working so hard to be acknowledged—dressed up in the easygoing "whatever" spirit of the inner teen.

Making Peace with Your Inner Teen

It's essential to create peace between the inner seven-year-old and the inner teen while protecting the vulnerability of the inner three-year-old. The inner teen is trying to keep us safe from our relentless, hard-working inner seven-year-old, and the inner seven-year-old cannot stand the inner teen who keeps hijacking us and trying to sabotage us from achieving our ideal outcomes. Go to **WWW.DrBeth.com/freestuff** for examples of inner family sabotage and the inner family chart. (You will also find other helpful parenting and personal resources there.)

The divine wise woman/wise man (the adult)

The divine wise self can be found by imagining your ideal, perfect parent or ideal mentor, and is also your future self. This is the part of you who is in closest connection to the Divine. Loving, positive, all-knowing, and spirit-driven, this self is unconditionally accepting of all, accepting of what is in any given moment, is relaxed and peaceful knowing everything is always perfect and divine (P&D). This self understands the big picture. This self is a visionary, present in the moment, generous with love and gratitude, meeting all internal needs abundantly, independently free, mature, selfless, self-loving, teachable, and open to learning. This sovereign self shares, owns, cleans up her/his own stuff with no competition, has undying faith, and knows that it is all P&D. :)

At the heart of the journey, you are trying to protect the inner three-year-old, your feelings, and your passions. When you can get to the heart of your soul and make your vulnerable inner three-year-old feel safe, then your inner seven-year-old will feel like they have done their job protecting your inner three-year-old, who can then "chill out" feeling accomplished. When your inner seven-year-old stops being so critical and judgmental, then your inner teen will feel free to fully and passionately express herself/himself.

When your inner teen collaborates, becomes a team player, explains why the acting-out behavior (e.g. over-spending, drinking, "checking out") has been happening, comes on board, and follows through, then the inner seven-year-old will feel safe and start to "chillax" and see the responsibility, benefits, and the importance of playing and relaxing. Then the inner teen, finally feeling heard, does not need to over-exaggerate and engage in destructive, self-sabotaging behaviors.

When the inner seven-year-old understands the power and benefit of allowing the inner teen to let off steam through playful, silly, irrational behavior, then everyone calms down, is on the same team, and is able to enjoy the moment. This is the foundation for a perfectly balanced life. We get to not only survive, but to truly thrive and live full out!

As you learn to recognize and listen to each of these emotional stepping stones—represented by the members of your inner family—each part will feel heard and understood. You will begin to feel unconditional love, compassion, and acceptance for *all* parts of yourself. Once all parts of you are living in peace and harmony, achieving your ideal outcomes becomes elegant and effortless.

One of the goals of defining and sharing your story with yourself and others is to come to a sense of wholeness, that sense of completeness you have always wanted. You are lovable and everything in your life is and always has been perfect and divine.

Now Let's Find Your Story

1. Get a piece of paper, a notepad, or your journal and write out all the things you don't like about yourself, your body, your family, your situation, your job, your friends, your life, etc. What's not working for you? Really let it rip!

2. Look for common threads. What are the negative beliefs/stories you have about yourself and others? Take special note of those things that don't even feel like beliefs, but are more like actual facts ("the truth").

3. Review the negative beliefs/stories and number them in order of importance. Number one has the greatest impact on you, the most

intense hook, charge, or trigger. (Hint: If you are triggered, it is yours to heal—ONLY if you want your power and love back!)

Be open and willing to get uncomfortable for a bit. I promise it won't hurt for long. The more you are willing to turn up the volume on your discomfort, the more rewarding your breakthrough will be. You may just get your ideal outcomes if you're willing to play full out!

What's your "not working" story? That's where this story ends and the next will begin . . .

What's your "not working" story? Here's one way you can write it out:

"I'm _____, which according to my beliefs and what others/ society have told me, means that_____."

Go to DrBeth's Double Dog Dare Community to join the group **https:// courses.drbethyou.com/community** and share your new/old story that you are ready to transform!

Go to **DrBeth.com/freestuff**:

<u>**You'll receive an email with access to these four gifts**</u>:

1. The report "Making It Fun to Get Things Done."
2. The book *Embracing Defiance: Helping Your Child Express Their Unique Voice While Keeping Your Sanity.*
3. The Power Parenting Quiz/Power Business Quiz.
4. Access to the Double Dog Dare Community.

If you have any questions about this process or would like any support finding your "not working story," click here to join my complimentary webinar, "What's Your Story?" Be ready to let go and enjoy the ride. And remember, there is no way to screw this up!

P.S. Don't forget to take great care of yourself first!

Dr. Beth :)

Beth Halbert

Dr. Beth Halbert, a.k.a. DrBeth, known as "America's Teenologist," has more than 30 years of experience working as a corporate trainer, keynote speaker, executive coach, educator, and consultant for family-owned businesses and Fortune 500 companies. She has a thriving private clinical psychology practice, facilitates national workshops for parents and teens, and delivers highly educational and extremely entertaining keynote presentations.

DrBeth is committed to creating sustainable social change and supporting people to become the leaders they want to be. Among her clients are American Family Insurance, Cadillac, General Motors, Honda, JD Power and Associates, Marriott, McGraw Hill, Toyota, and Volkswagen. She has also been featured on more than 200 nationally syndicated television, radio, newspaper, and magazine outlets.

As a licensed child psychologist and expert with teens, parents, teachers, health professionals, and others, DrBeth has worked with thousands of families and "first responders" to create stronger parent-teen bonds. She takes a unique approach to helping families overcome the difficulties of adolescence, combining proven clinical practices with warmth, playfulness, self-expression, love, and compassion. She knows how teens think and act and gets them to talk about their emotions and behaviors. She also knows strong-willed adults and gets them to accept themselves exactly as they are and accept their children and others exactly as they are.

In short, DrBeth fully understands human behavior, relational dynamics, and "inner family" dynamics (including our inner three-year-old's, our inner seven-year-old's, and our inner teen's dynamics). She works closely and compassionately with people of all ages, supporting them to appreciate themselves, engage in positive dialogue with others, and develop healthy, connected, loving relationships in especially challenging, dysfunctional situations.

Email Address: **DrBeth@DrBeth.com**
Cell Phone Number: (925) 403-4113 (textable)
Website: **DrBeth.com**
Facebook page(s):
www.facebook.com/drbethcp
https://www.facebook.com/DrBethTeenologist/
https://www.facebook.com/groups/1498857563603184 (Double
Dog Dare Challenge group)
LinkedIn page: **https://www.linkedin.com/in/drbeth/**
Twitter handle: DrBethCP **http://twitter.com/DrBethCP**
YouTube Channel: DrBethCP **www.youtube.com/user/drbethcp**
Other Social Media Channels:
Instagram: DrBethH: **https://www.instagram.com/drbethh/**
Pinterest: DrBethCP: **https://www.pinterest.com/drbethcp/_saved/**

UPGRADE YOUR HABITS FOR SELF-CARE
BY TRACIE ROOT

The basis of self-care is to CARE for your SELF.

I learned true self-care only after there was nobody left but myself to care for me. Grief and the aftermath taught me to notice what I needed to do so I could move beyond survival. I learned to thrive. It took a while.

Our kids were two and four when Paul died. For four years, I spent my time learning how to keep two babies alive, and him too, for a while. He went through chemo, radiation, remission, recurrence, and ultimately passed in May of 2010. It was intense. I had some support during his illness, but most of our family lived far away. I had some friends who came to help when I cried out, but that was exhausting for me. I didn't know how to ask for support and I didn't know how to take it when it was offered unexpectedly.

A kind woman at our church offered to help by cooking some meals for me and the kids, and I turned her down flat. I was embarrassed to admit any lack of control over our situation. I'll never forget that moment. Thankfully, it stuck with me so I could learn from it.

After about a year and a half, I started to come out of the fog of grief. I realized I needed to make decisions for myself, so I could be better, feel better, and do better for my kids and for our future. When what's possible is all the shades of gray, life can be overwhelming. I finally chose the light.

Why are we so willing to let go of things that feel hard? It's not even that they are hard, but right now they feel hard. We want easy. Comfortable. Convenient. We want success without even trying. (Wasn't there a movie with that title?) **Our whole lives we've wanted to succeed without even trying. BUT it's in the trying that we succeed. It's not about the end game, it's about the process.**

I didn't know why what I had tried in my past hadn't worked to change my health and well-being permanently. Didn't I already know what to do for myself, my energy, my weight, and my future? I was smart, but I was lost, without direction. I trusted the universe to send me new ideas and new methods.

I paid attention, tried new things, and I found a way to start. I accepted a tiny bit of help in the form of a physician-led weight loss program with a free health coach, a bunch of people online to talk to. In doing so, I learned what I didn't know that I didn't know. It gave me the structure I didn't know I needed. I got to a healthy weight quickly and—while my journey started by looking for a way to change my physical shape, my energy, and my self-esteem—what I actually learned were new *habits of the mind* that helped me make new and positive decisions for myself every day. It empowered me to choose myself and to consider living life differently.

We are empowered in all things, but we have to take it. Accept empowerment as our truth. Know, and then, tell others—they might not know it yet. I think, behave, manage, take actions, and make decisions toward my goal. I own my personal authority to do what matters to me. That's empowerment, the physical and the mental. As if they were not connected!

It's exciting to watch and experience the interconnectedness of the universe and the beings within it—the energy everything emits. Relax physically and you'll mentally be more relaxed too. There's also the identity factor in this. If you are embarrassed by something, you will be less engaged, even if you're interested. If fear stops you, how will you continue? If you tell yourself you are or aren't something, or "that person," then you're right. Someone who identifies themselves as a giver, a nurturer, someone who is other-focused, may have a story in their head that this makes them good and virtuous, and that's what's right, what they were taught. And if they act in a way that's contrary to that, it makes them a bad person. What happens if you're perceived (by yourself) as a bad person? Then nobody will like you. You'll be an outcast, and in a tribal society, that is death. So, we please. We do for others, so we will be accepted. We achieve, so we'll be admired. We win, so we're the strongest of the tribe and our bloodline lives on. These tendencies are deep in our psyche and in our past!

Everything is a choice, and I have the power to choose. I must care for myself in order to be my best for others.

Self-care looks totally different to each of us. It's not only massage and nail appointments, even though those are certainly some of my favorites! It also looks like:

Rest. Introspection. Patience. Nutritious food. Moderation. Acknowledgement. Confidence. Water. Grace.

It's the empowered choices we make in support of ourselves that matter, that keep us on the healthy track, that fuel our bodies, souls, and minds.

After almost a decade of coaching people on their health and weight loss goals, I have found there to be five key areas where, if we upgrade our current habits even a little bit, we will be ready and on the way to a better, healthier, more energetic, and more vibrant life. These qualities in a body lead to the qualities of the mind that can uplift and empower ourselves and others. Confidence, clarity, and the ability to step through and past challenges to get where we are dreaming about going! These five habits seem physical, but watch for the similarities on how they affect the brain and our mental health, too!

Five Habits to Upgrade Your Self-Care

1. Water

As a young person, I lived on caffeine and nicotine. When I was in the high school marching band as a freshman, the older kids brought their morning Tab soda with them. I adopted this habit because I liked the taste, I liked those kids, and wanted to feel included. It was funny to talk about caffeine as a way of life, a "safe" drug.

Caffeine was my drug of choice, until I turned 19 and started smoking cigarettes. There it was, the caffeine and nicotine lifestyle. I knew it was unhealthy, but who cared. I was a young beautiful woman in the 80's and 90's, and a fast lifestyle was fun without being too out of hand with anything more illicit. I didn't break that pack-a-day smoking habit until 17 years later when I found out I was (unknowingly) pregnant with our first child. I'm forever grateful for the morning sickness that seemed to be triggered whenever I lit up. Once I confirmed I was having a baby, I gave those cancer sticks up for good without a struggle.

After the kids were born and I began looking at my unhealthy lifestyle, I realized that I drank coffee, diet soda, and wine—and little else. I started drinking water during the work day, after my beloved morning coffee. The diet soda was my "treat" after I consumed 100 ounces of water. It was a great start to a habit I've built, improved, and kept up for over eight years now. (*Sips water while typing this chapter.)

2. Sleep

The mantra of the 80's, of high-achievers, of coffee-lovers . . . "I'll sleep when I'm dead."

I woke up, caffeinated myself, worked, achieved, lived in the moment, and went to bed late at night. I was a night owl even though I was waking up at 6 am for my morning commute, which took anywhere from an hour to two hours, depending on the client and where I lived at the time. This is what life was like in Silicon Valley. I'd been grooming myself for it ever since I was a child: work hard, go to college, get a great job, climb the ladder, and if you're good enough, tap on the glass ceiling.

I was notoriously under slept, although, because I was young, I believed it didn't matter. Because it was a fun life, I wasn't about to change anything. I didn't connect it to my obesity. I didn't connect it to my smoking habit, or my sugar and caffeine cravings. I was constantly looking for the next "hit" to keep up my energy so I didn't feel exhausted.

If we let our self-care fall, our energy, clarity, commitment, and spirit all fall. Get your sleep, folks.

3. Activity

Notice, I didn't say "exercise." Activity doesn't have to be what we have been fed from the Jack LaLane and Jazzercise days. Structured exercise is great and so beneficial—but what if you have bad knees? What if you have asthma? It can be hard to get started because we "think" we have to do way more than we need to in order to begin.

Being an active person creates happy chemicals in our brains. Expending this energy creates more energy in our bodies. It will also:

- Promote cardiovascular health.
- Improve blood flow to the brain.
- Reduce inflammation.
- Lower levels of stress hormones.

There may be physical benefits to the brain, too, such as improving the nerve fibers that connect the brain's nerve-cell-rich gray matter. It also promotes neuroplasticity, which affects our ability to adapt to unexpected situations and experiences in our lives. Ultimately, incorporating some level of healthy motion in our lives is crucial to long-term physical and mental health.

4. Breath

Back in those younger days, I didn't exercise and I smoked, so breathing deeply included inhaling chemicals that were slowly poisoning me. I knew our cells needed oxygen and that it was through our breath that oxygen was carried via our blood to our whole body. But again, who cared? And yes, the brain needs blood and oxygen, but wasn't that what yawning did for us? Bring oxygen to the brain? Well I rarely yawned because I wasn't tired due to the caffeination and all the nicotine, so I didn't notice how exhausted I was. I didn't learn how learning to take deep, cleansing breaths could not only improve me physically, but also mentally, and especially emotionally. It was only a few years ago when I realized how unconscious I was about the use of the breath to enhance calm and increase focus. Three deep, long breaths can literally change your brain chemistry and you can start anew on the task at hand or the conversation in progress.

5. Grace

I was a perfectionist. As a performer (music, dance, there was always a show to put on), the goal was always to be perfect, look perfect, and show up perfectly. My fellow performers and I were a team, and a synchronous performance from the ensemble was what won prizes—and we won LOTS of prizes. Practically all the prizes. So, perfection was always the expectation. I was also a high-achiever in school and school was easy. If I applied myself at all, straight A's came easy. But who cared? I didn't have big goals in life. I didn't want to be a doctor, or a lawyer, or even a teacher. I just wanted to live in the moment, perform, have fun, and be noticed for my perfection.

I learned that perfection is unattainable. Literally, it's not possible to be perfect in life. In practically anything you can imagine there is room for improvement. Once I stopped expecting perfection of myself, things got a lot more peaceful inside me. And when I stopped expecting perfection of others, things got a lot more peaceful around me. **Practice and progress, not perfection.**

I am a recovering perfectionist. I have deep-seated, high-level personal expectations, which means I am constantly telling myself that it's not only OK, but better to give myself and others grace. Practice and progress, not perfection.

Upgrading these five areas of my life—my body and mind, my thoughts and habits, my self-care—this is what I began to learn in 2012 and have been practicing ever since. **Empowerment is self-leadership. We choose. We decide. We are in control of our own choices. That's the definition of empowerment.**

Tracie Root

Tracie Root is a coach, a speaker, an educator, and a community builder.

Tracie ended her career in corporate America and found her new calling after a family tragedy. Her partner of almost 20 years passed away after a battle with cancer at the age of 47. Tracie and her two toddlers were left with no family nearby, a house "under water" from the housing crisis, and she couldn't see how anything was going to change. Ever.

Then, years later—a spark. That light inside her, dimmed after years of trauma and loss, began to shine brighter. She saw a way back to her former self and began the journey, one step at a time. She shifted her career to one of helping others at a deeper level while making more time for her own fulfillment, adventure, and joy.

Now Tracie helps women remember their best selves. For almost a decade, she's been serving and supporting clients around the country to SET and to GET their goals in health, life, and business. With the founding of Gather in 2019 and its expansion in 2020, she took her own goal-getting advice and created a community of like-minded women who are growing and thriving together. Tracie coaches people around the country, one-on-one and in groups, to help them move from feeling stuck to shining bright, so they can be bolder and brighter, live in their authentic truth, and THRIVE.

Tracie is an engaging and enthusiastic speaker. Audience members take away the belief that they can do ANYTHING! Tracie speaks frequently on cultivating optimal health and well-being, goal-setting and strategy, entrepreneurship, overcoming tragedy and loss, and other personal development topics.

Tracie lives in Santa Cruz, CA and is married to her best friend. Together they are raising two teens and a dog.

Email: **Tracie@TracieRoot.com**
Phone: (408) 687-0765
Website: **https://www.TracieRoot.com**
Facebook: **https://www.facebook.com/tracie.tree.root**
Facebook: **https://www.facebook.com/tracieroot.coaching**
Facebook: **https://www.facebook.com/gatherinsantacruz**
LinkedIn: **https://www.linkedin.com/in/tracieroot**
YouTube Channel: **https://www.youtube.com/channel/UCkhaq-InBWFQ6Ll8EzABlIw**
Instagram: **https://www.instagram.com/tracieroot_coaching**
Instagram: **https://www.instagram.com/gatherinsantacruz**

EMPOWERED CHOICE:
SELF-CARE AS A WAY OF BEING
BY KAREN EISCHEN AND MEL PERRY

On my 50th Birthday, I was spending an idyllic day with my daughter Mel and husband Dennis. We were on a crisp white mountain top with the sun shining in an azure blue sky. I had the best life I could have imagined: a loving husband with whom I'd spent 31 wonderful years, a beautiful daughter about to graduate high school, and a great career that provided financial security. **My life was taking a trajectory I had planned.**

A few weeks later, Dennis and I were talking about the upcoming week. One moment he was sitting on the bed talking about the day. In the next breath he said, "I'm tired," and in another, Dennis was gone. I had never thought about a life without him so soon. **I was blindsided. I had not made plans or thought about what my life would be like without him. My world had been turned upside down.**

Everything changed in a moment. I did not know what to do next, except to get up out of bed every day. Doing my corporate consulting job on autopilot became a safe routine to get through my day. I had disengaged with my purpose. I continued on this path for a couple of years, putting one foot in front of the other. I had very little joy in my life besides my daughter.

Then, the Universe nudged me. There was a downturn in the corporation. They chose to lay me off. I was left with a future of unknowns.

After I lost my husband, my retirement dreams had shattered.

And, after losing my job, I was left with a blank canvas called the future.

Faced with a lot of time, it was time to take down the walls of what was possible for myself and my future.

I had a choice.

I gave myself permission and space to go within, to dream, to ask deep questions, and be with the answers my soul was trying to tell me that I had been too busy to hear before.

I learned to live in the moment and know that there is an opportunity to welcome joy into life, each and every day.

Standing on the mountain top on that perfect early spring day, my mind had been filled with worry. I could have had much more joy in the days we had together versus putting off dreams until the right time.

On my journey, I was forced to face my blank canvas.

You, too, can choose to take five minutes a day to slow down and sit with the quiet. You do not have to wait for a loss, a challenge, or life to change on you. You can choose to be still and listen now.

Our intuition is always here, waiting to guide us, but it needs space and quiet for us to hear it. **I encourage you to get back in touch with you.** You deserve a life that you absolutely love waking up to in the morning. You can create a life that is joyful now, as well as for whatever your future may hold.

Being on purpose, making a positive difference with your gifts, and building a legacy, is a marathon, not a sprint. It is a journey.

We believe you have a message and a contribution to make in this world that requires you to nurture your body, mind, and spirit, so that you can show up. You owe it to yourself and to those you are meant to serve to prioritize you and live in an intentional state of self-love.

Self-care is a way of being, rooted in empowered choices, and is absolutely critical for success.

Choose to Step Forward

Even with the best tools and strategies available, you may still not implement, make time, and have great excuses. Why? We believe the root is worthiness. **If, at your core, you don't feel worthy of joy and your dreams, you will run out of time for self-care. You won't do it.**

For years, social anxiety ruled Mel's life. It controlled me. I locked myself away from the world because I was afraid of being hurt. I shut the world out. In shutting the world out, I shut down.

My struggles with debilitating social anxiety had me lay awake in silent midnight hours, telling myself that tomorrow would be different. Day, after month, after year faded away with the same midnight wish until I decided that the greatest fear was wasting my life and hiding away from the world. Then, I took the even scarier step to reach out.

When I took a tiny step, it built my confidence, so I was willing to take another tiny step, building and building. Over the years, I did a lot of work to get to the place where I am now, thriving instead of just surviving. As I cultivated my self, belief, and confidence, I was able to see how worthy I was to live the life of my dreams.

You can choose to lean into anxiety, overwhelm and busy yourself, or do whatever else is keeping you from your best life, or you can lean into joy, possibility, love, and potential. At any moment, you choose. When I chose joy, everything opened up.

At first, it took a lot of intentional effort for me to say I'm going to choose the positive, and it did not last long. As confidence became a muscle, where I stretched into my potential, I was able to stay in that state longer and longer. Now, joy has become a way of being.

I am not the same person that I used to be. I am much more than I ever thought I could be. And there is so much more potential and possibility for all of us. The first step is choice.

Declare that you are worthy and prove it to yourself. Start by writing down all of the things that you have done and have in your life. It is important to really see that you have done a lot. You have accomplished big things. You are successful. You already have what it takes to create what you want in this world.

You have a purpose and a reason to serve. Your experiences are your resources. You have been through a journey that could serve somebody else. When helping yourself, you create tools that become your toolbox. You can share this toolbox with others.

You have everything inside of you. It is important to ground yourself into knowing that you are enough, and then take tiny steps. And when you have the tools to know you are worthy, then you start attracting the success, impact, and legacy you desire. **It starts with choosing you and then creating the plan.**

Tiny steps add up and propel you forward. As you step forward, you will rise up and shine.

Choose Your Focus

You can design your life in such a way that you can welcome joy every day no matter what ups and downs you may encounter. To do this, **get clear about what is most important and prioritize those on your calendar.** When you invest your time connected to your vision, you make progress towards your most important goals without feeling overwhelmed. You can enjoy your life and the process of pursuing the things that light you up.

Plan for your week ahead, focus on the Three Big Goals that will move you forward. Start your morning with one intention that you know you can successfully accomplish and end the day with a "Ta-Da!" list.

Celebrate the things you did do. Write these down. A single step is worth celebrating. **Focusing on moving the needle forward will take the**

focus off the overwhelmingly big picture. You get to enjoy the journey every day.

Choose Your Energy

In my corporate career, with over 25 years of project management and performance training, I consulted over 1000 employees from the manufacturing floor to the C-suite. My role evolved to supporting others in powerfully choosing and embodying self-care, on and off the job. **I discovered that, to thrive in your business and life, the foundation for success needs to include leading from self-love, prioritizing you, and non-negotiable self-care.**

Yet, as busy women with seemingly endless lists of to-dos, self-care and self-love can take the back burner. We've learned that when self-care takes the back burner, we burn out. **Getting knocked out can be such a wake up call.**

When our business got busy, with too much to do and not enough time, my head filled with deadlines and producing results. When we got slammed, my self-care breaks blended together with work, overwhelming us.

In the midst of doing our virtual empowerment summit, I got what I thought was food poisoning. I was actually having a gallbladder attack. I was in bed for two weeks.

Because I had the systems and structure in place, my business could run without me. I took the time to slow down and return to the practices that I thought I could leave off my plate while I was busy. I got back to where I could be that vibrant leader.

To sustain your business, you need to sustain yourself.

I started with short intentional walks with our dog Maizie. As she lived in the present moment, so did I. These morning walks became a form of meditation. An opportunity to start the day grounded, rooted in love.

A simple step is to be more intentional with something that you already like to do, make that an intentional habit. Then, prioritize it on your calendar. What gets on your calendar gets done. Self-care and self-love need to be on your calendar so it becomes a non-negotiable. Five minutes can make a big difference in how you show up for the rest of your day. Decide what nourishes you. The simpler, the better.

There are a lot of things coming at us, which can, if we don't have a solid foundation of self-care, knock us out, out of what we want to do and what we're here to do.

Your dreams and business cannot work unless you do.

In order to stay in it, we need empowered choices to fuel us. You get to choose you first so that you can be a positive force in this world.

Choose Your State

How you show up is so important. Start with how you show up for yourself.

To walk through my social anxiety and to shine with confidence and joy, I intentionally reprogrammed the messages that my brain was telling me. One way is writing "I Love You" and "Me First" on sticky notes and post them all over the house. Creating as many spaces for this message to be seen. A favorite place is the mirror.

At first, I struggled with positive self-talk so I started playing what we now call "I love you" songs. Songs with messages that invite you into a positive state, especially when you're unable to do that for yourself. Lean on the vision of others to enlighten yourself. Music also gets you moving. You may have noticed that when animals get stressed, they shake off to release the energy. Research shows we also benefit from movement. It takes less than a minute for energy to shift.

The next step is to recognize and acknowledge that you are fabulous right now. When you walk into a room, including virtually, say to yourself, "You are fabulous! I love you! People are attracted to you!" It will change how you show up. **When you walk into a room, entering with positive messaging shifts your energy. People will naturally be drawn into your light and love.**

Get into state. Prioritize intentionally loving yourself more. Start with what you can sustain right now. While getting ready, make it part of your morning routine. Start with five minutes. Commit to the rituals that will have you falling in love with yourself. When you do, you attract abundance.

Choose Your Circle

Choosing how, where, and with whom you spend your energy will support you in your journey to welcoming more joy and empowered choice.

Studies show that if you surround yourself with positive people, positive thoughts, positive thinking, it will rub off on you. Those around you can uplift you, or they can easily drag you down. And it does not matter how strong you are inside, eventually, the world will influence you. This is why it's also important to not go it alone.

You already have what it takes to create what you want and having support creates momentum. When you are with others that are living on purpose with purpose, it elevates your purpose. It grounds you, you shine brighter when you are with people that are shining bright themselves. Surrounding yourself with others with big dreams, awakens the possibilities within and taps into your limitless potential. Women coming together to choose love and joy for themselves is the starting point for future possibilities for women worldwide.

When we found our community of like hearted and like-minded women, our dreams, goals, and aspirations grew. On each step of our uncharted journey, we were lifted up by women who had gone before us, who said, "yes, it is possible, keep going." We found a safe container to build our business and life, so we could wake up with joy.

When you are grounded in your worthiness, you have a solid foundation built on loving yourself first, you are showing up and you are shining bright, you can confidently choose the rooms you enter as well as leave those that no longer serve you.

Choose Joy

Through our pain blossomed joy.

We choose to share our stories, our experiences, and our journey as tools to support other women.

We founded our coaching company, Envision Joy Today™, out of a longing for women to love their lives now, and not to wait for a certain milestone, a certain achievement, or a certain number in their bank account, before saying, "I can have joy and now I can do that." The best day to step into all that you are meant to be, do, and have is today, RIGHT NOW!

It is time to break through. Let go of what's been holding you back, keeping you playing small in your life and your business, and what no longer serves you.

There is freedom in progress. As you step forward, your confidence to stay on track increases. When things get off track, when obstacles arise, and when challenges come about, you will be able to navigate.

The version of you that you dream about is absolutely possible. And, it's all on the other side of choosing you, showing up, creating the systems and strategies for success your way, and reaching out to those who can help you get there!

It's time to say yes! Say yes to you, yes to possibility, and yes to joy.

Love, lead, and live your life to the fullest!

Karen Eischen and Mel Perry

Creatives, leaders, and visionary women partner with Karen Eischen and Mel Perry to amplify their calling, align their magnetizing message with a sustainable plan they can trust, and let go of what is holding them back, so they can grow their communities, attract their dream clients, and make a positive difference in a fun and fulfilling way.

A mom and daughter team, Karen and Mel are empowered leadership coaches and visibility strategists with 50 years of combined experience. Together, they support women to step up, stand out, and shine bright as authentic leaders with clarity, consistency, and confidence, finally leaving the frustration and burn out behind.

With a focus on project management, performance, and leadership, Karen has consulted over a 1000 people to powerfully prioritize self-love and embody self-care, on and off the job.

After struggling with social anxiety for years, Mel surrounded herself with powerful healers, and, with tiny steps, grew to shine. She now combines her years in stage performance with her personal development toolkit to focus on presence, messaging, and confidence.

As producers and co-hosts of virtual events for women, Karen and Mel share the stage with women worldwide. They are known for creating spaces where women have the opportunity to shine. Their latest project, Shine the Spotlight on You, won a BOVE (Best Of Virtual Events) award. And, they are contributing authors in the *Empowering CEOs* book project.

Karen and Mel founded their coaching company, Envision Joy Today™, out of a longing for women to love their lives now and empower women to change the world with mission-led businesses. They invite you to love, lead, and live to the fullest every day with a business that fits YOU, that aligns with your life, and brings fulfillment and joy. It's time for success your way!

We invite you to connect with us:
Email: **karenandmel@envisionjoytoday.com**
Website: **www.envisionjoytoday.com/ILoveYouGift**
Facebook Page: **www.facebook.com/envisionjoytoday**
Radiant Women In Business Connect Facebook Group:
www.facebook.com/groups/radiantwomeninbusinessconnect
Karen Eischen LinkedIn:
www.linkedin.com/in/karen-eischen-envision-joy-today
Mel Perry LinkedIn: **www.linkedin.com/in/mel-perry-ejt**
YouTube Channel: @envisionjoytoday
Tik Tok: @envisionjoytoday
Instagram: @envisionjoytoday

THE ART OF EMBODIED SELF-CARE
BY MICHELLE MAREE

Recently, more recently than I would like to admit, I had a significant panic attack.

Despite my knowledge of anxiety and panic disorders and decades of work with them, I was terrified. I was so sure I was experiencing anaphylaxis after having eaten some shellfish. (Despite the fact that I've eaten shellfish before and never had any kind of reaction.) My throat was tight, I felt pressure in my chest, my hands were cold, my heart was racing. I felt like I was going to pass out, lose control or even die, and I kept repeating tearfully to my husband "I'm so sorry. I don't know what to do. I'm so sorry." I had lost connection with my own body, and was being ruled by my nervous system.

When I looked back, I realized that many of my self-care practices had simply slid by the wayside without my awareness. As I, and so many other providers, rushed to support clients who were struggling through this very difficult time in our history, **I had forgotten to practice what I preach.**

That's a really hard thing for me to admit. I am a psychotherapist, a transformational coach, speaker, and change agent, and the subject I speak most often about is . . . dun dun dun dun . . . _self-care_.

Believe me, I could write a whole chapter on the inner-dialogue that occurred before I started writing this chapter on self-care. I could tell you about every judgmental thought that I've had about myself as an expert on this subject.

Instead, I'm going to ask you to meditate on the phrase, "We teach what we seek to master." I seek to master the art of self-care. In fact, having a panic attack at this stage in my career and mastery is exactly why I need to write this chapter, and why much of my work is now focused on supporting feminine leaders in making self-care non-negotiable.

Why do mechanics often have crappy cars? They tinker and play and modify their cars, but the bulk of their mastery is usually focused on others. It's often how they make a living. Sometimes it's related to their self-esteem. Somehow doing it for themselves just isn't the same. There is nothing quite like seeing and experiencing the gratitude of someone who has benefited from your mastery. It feels good to our souls. We feel fulfilled, proud, accomplished, and acknowledged for the skills that we have honed.

Sound familiar?

Many practitioners, clinicians, and thought leaders spend a lot of focus and energy on others. We share what we know freely. We love to serve.

The question becomes, how good are we at serving ourselves?

I like to use the example of a fountain when talking about self-care. If there is no water in the bottom of the fountain, it has nothing to give. Sure, it might sputter out some mud or dust, but nothing really useful. It is only when the bottom of the fountain is full that the fountain can actually be effective, beautiful, and bountiful.

The bottom of the fountain are the tools, activities, and mindsets that we choose on a regular basis to keep our fountain full, so that we are giving from a place of abundance. We are giving from our overflow, rather than from the bare minimum needed to make the fountain work.

Trauma and self-care: Engaging in self-care can become extra challenging when you have a history of trauma. Trauma is something people don't like to talk about, and yet many of the therapists, coaches, and healing practitioners that I know have experienced trauma.

For those with a trauma history, there is an added barrier to actually engaging in and enjoying the art of self-care. Self-care can seem like a luxury that they can't afford because their attention and energy has been trained to be so focused on survival, self-protection, or caretaking others. Sometimes the barrier is that self-care wasn't modeled because caretakers were also trauma survivors, or maybe even berated for their attempts to engage in self-care. I know many service providers and clinicians who have turned their trauma into their triumph, and pass on their knowledge to others to support them in the way that they wish they had been supported. I also know that for them, self-care, especially embodied self-care, can be very challenging.

Embodiment and self-care: Simply put, embodiment is the ability to be completely present in the moment, aware of body sensations, feelings, and thoughts all at the same time, without shutting down or becoming reactive. This is the ultimate goal of any trauma survivor. Really, it's the ultimate goal for any of us who want to stay present with others in our lives. We want to be able to engage in challenging conversations with grace. We do not want to be ruled by our nervous system, old trauma responses, or inaccurate perceptions. We want to model for our children how to manage strong emotions, stressful events, and everyday inconveniences in a way that inspires hope and gratitude. We want to be able to hold deep and sacred space for those who are struggling.

One can be a very physical person and not be embodied. I know athletes who can't feel their feelings. Seasoned meditators who scream at their spouses or children when they're upset or triggered. I've spent years working with individuals who have disordered eating. They may be very active WITH their bodies, but they are not comfortable IN their bodies. Many of them are unable to tell me how they feel, or tell me that their feelings overwhelm them so they do everything they can to avoid feeling them. For many of us, it is like there is this separation between our heads and our bodies.

So, why do I put so much focus on embodiment in self-care? I've spent the last 15 years immersed in the field of trauma work. As the field of trauma-informed care has evolved, there is one aspect that stands out as a core skill that is needed for true, deep, and lasting healing. That skill is embodiment

I am a trauma thriver. I am a service provider who has come through to the other side of trauma and have spent my life supporting others

through theirs. Embodiment practices brought me back home to myself. They were pivotal in not only my own healing, but in my capacity to support others in their healing. Embodiment improved my relationships, my confidence, my ability to experience pleasure, my awareness, my sense of presence, my groundedness, and my ability to show up fully as my unique, vulnerable, and authentic self.

I used to believe that my body was an unsafe place to be. I went from one extreme to the other. I participated in over exercising, numbing myself with food, ignoring body sensations (like hunger and that I had to pee), body shame, and avoidance of the very things I knew would help me reconnect to my body. Once I began learning about and practicing embodiment exercises, I found a sense of awe and freedom in my body that I had never experienced before. **I discovered that the reality was, being IN my body was the SAFEST place I could be.** When I stayed in my body during arguments or distressing events, I felt more in control, less "wobbly," and I was able to be more present and fully engage in the moment. I became unshakeable—like a strong tree that can flexibly bend with the wind, but nothing can shake its foundation.

Embodiment is the bridge between the power of the mind and the wisdom of the body.

When we know how to be embodied, we can slow down time, take a slight step back, and observe what is happening within and around us. When we come from an embodied place—rather than numbing out, avoiding, or exploding—we can be grounded, connected, aware, and able to be with our feelings safely.

For those who provide support for the healing of others, being embodied is a super power that enhances all of the skills you already have. It allows you to feel into what your client may be experiencing without losing yourself in it, taking it on, or acting it out later. We can also get triggered by our children, other family members, and our partners. Learning how to stay embodied despite the distress you are feeling can do wonders for increasing deep connection, empathy, and effectiveness while caring for others. Practicing embodied self-care allows you to keep coming back to the table, fully alive, fully present, and fully engaged. For trauma survivors this is a skill that needs to be built slowly, consciously, and with care.

If we are not IN our bodies, our self-care is less effective. When we practice any kind of self-care and we aren't present, how effective was it really? How many times have you gone to do something with the intention of it being relaxing, only to find that you didn't actually give yourself the opportunity to experience it? Maybe you were "thinking too much," kept getting distracted by your phone, the kids. or other "tasks." When we are embodied, it is like we soak up every ounce of an experience and it goes into our self-care fountain and creates energy for future use. Embodiment is a core component of self-care.

There are four quadrants that are helpful to look at when practicing your own self-care.

Physical, Emotional, Mental and Spiritual

Physical: Health, beauty, sexuality, energy, nourishment, physical movement, etc.

Emotional: healthy and grounded expression, naming and processing feelings, releasing emotional energy, experiencing sensations, etc.

Mental: thoughts, perceptions, beliefs, stories/narratives, education, structures, etc.

Spiritual: prayer, mindfulness, meditation, nature-based practices, etc.

Many of us know that it is important to exercise, drink plenty of water, practice good hygiene, eat whole foods, get regular physical health check-ups, and practice mindfulness to calm our brains and regulate our systems. We've also learned that community and believing in something greater than ourselves can help us put things into perspective in a way that we just can't when we're locked inside our own minds.

So, why is it that many of us still suck at regularly practicing self-care in these areas?

Many of us keep our greatest self-care ideas in our heads. We don't actually do them, or we do them sporadically when the inspiration hits us. Many of us do not have a consistent and effective self-care plan or "practice." We often convince ourselves that we will do it later, that something else is more important right now, or that it's just going to take too much effort.

I've discovered, over decades of supporting people to reach their physical, emotional, mental, and spiritual goals that there are six keys we need to focus on in each area of self-care in order to ensure the effective creation and implementation of a regular practice.

The six keys to "effective" self-care: **Motivation, expectation, intention, mindfulness, self-discipline, and practice.**

Self-care isn't all bubble baths and spa days. When we have loose ends in our lives they can become energy sappers, and sometimes the best self-care we can do is to take care of business (paying bills, cleaning out a space, returning that impulse buy), so that we have more energy to focus on the things we enjoy.

Remember the image of the fountain. Self-care is anything that helps us regain vitality and energy so that we can be of service and do the things that we enjoy with as much presence as possible.

Motivation: *The more we focus on why we are motivated to make a change and the feelings we want to experience, the more our brain searches for opportunities to provide just that.*

Expectations: *When we set realistic expectations and stay present to our progress—rather than wishing for it to be something that it isn't—and when we can practice radical acceptance for where we are and what we are doing about it, we feel much better about the progress that we've made.*

Intention*: How we set ourselves up to engage in our self-care practices and keep our focus aligned with our goals on a deeper level. Intention is a loving act of accountability to oneself.*

Mindfulness: *Mindfulness is simply the ability to stay present and to participate fully in the moment. It requires focused attention and a desire to turn away from anything that distracts us from the present moment.*

Self-discipline*: Taking consistent action to create that which we desire despite distractions. Thinking about self-care and dreaming about self-care is not practicing self-care.*

The final, and dare I say most important key, is **practice**.

Have you ever learned something and understood it intellectually, but when it came time to actually do it got super nervous and lost your confidence or couldn't remember the steps? That is likely because you hadn't embodied the practice yet. One of my instructors in graduate school said that it takes 10 years to build mastery in a particular skill, and the reason for that is because you have to actively engage with the skill in order to build mastery in it. You can't reach mastery of a skill if it stays in the intellectual realm.

In order for us to become masters in self-care, we have to practice all of the above-mentioned pieces of the puzzle. We have to take *accountable action* and do it. We have to get clear on our *motivation* for doing it. We have to set reasonable *expectations* and change things up when necessary to keep it interesting. We have to set clear *intentions* so that we can know when we are on track and when we are off track. We need to be *mindful* of how we feel, noticing the messages that our bodies are sending us, identifying the thoughts and judgments that might be getting in our way and *fully engaging* in the present moment with all of our senses.

Creating a conscious connection between your mind and your body is an act of self-love and self-care. It helps you stay aware of what fills your fountain and what drains it. It also allows you to stand your ground more effectively, to speak your truth, to withstand the projections and judgments of others, to respond with grace, and to simply enjoy life more fully.

If you would like to explore the six keys (motivation, expectations, intention, mindfulness, self-discipline, and practice) further, please go and take my "Self-Care Effectiveness Assessment" at **www.michellemaree. com/Self-CareEffectivenessAssessment**. Here you will find questions you can ask yourself in each area to get crystal clear on what you need to do to make your plan effective, sustainable, and impactful.

Take a moment and write down any nuggets that can be applied to your own self-care. Where do you need to beef up your self-care? Where do you feel you're already doing pretty well? Is there anything that stood out as an important puzzle piece that's been missing for you in your self-care?

Create a plan around that.

Remember, it's called a self-care "practice." Practice means we get to make mistakes. We get to change our minds. We get to tweak it and try to make it better. We get to engage our curiosity and really feel into what's working for us and what isn't.

Many Blessings on your self-care journey,
Michelle Maree

Michelle Maree

Michelle Maree helps influential women show up powerfully, authentically, and unapologetically so they can create the impact and influence they truly desire, and KNOW they are here to make. She helps them breakthrough whatever barriers remain that may be keeping them on the hamster wheel of self-doubt, imposter syndrome, and playing it "safe."

Michelle blends her expertise in theatre and performance, psychotherapy, embodiment, speaker training, and transformational coaching to help women go deep and rediscover their unique magic so they can embody it, share it and profit from it.

Playing at the deep end of the pool, holding space for play, emotion and inquiry, and sensing what gifts lie beneath the surface are Michelle's superpowers. She is down to earth, playful, practical, transparent, vulnerable, direct and practices what she preaches.

Email Address: **michelle@michellemaree.com**
Phone Number: (707) 387-0167
Website: **https://michellemaree.com**
Facebook page(s): **https://www.facebook. com/womenofimpactandinfluence/ https://www.facebook.com/TraumaSpecialistHeartWhisperer/**
LinkedIn Page: **https://www.linkedin.com/ in/michelle-hardeman-guptill**
YouTube Channel: **https://youtube.com/ channel/UCd9ljCistiFqlVDMNTjAv2g**
Tiktok: **tiktok.com/**@michelle.maree

LEAN INTO DISCOMFORT
BY KELSEY BASSANINI

A sudden gust of wind snatched the beach umbrella from its sandy anchor and launched it into the side of the Jeep. The hollow metal pop startled everyone, and we instinctively ducked our heads. As soon as the adults realized the near fatal miss, they jumped up and secured all possible metal picnic objects from becoming projectiles. My father examined the side of the Jeep, and was relieved that the metal stem of the umbrella had not ruptured the gas tank. In the middle of this scene of excitement and confusion, no one kept an eye on a five-year-old girl who drifted off from shore on an inflatable beach mattress.

This was my first memory of my childhood in Vietnam. As I floated out to sea on that hot summer day, I did not feel afraid. My father finally swam out to get me. As he neared the inflatable mattress, I got so excited that I fell into the water, and I remember the feel of seaweed catching my fall until my father could reach me. As an adult revisiting my childhood memory, I find it remarkable that I had no fear of the ocean. My child's instinct knew I was being beckoned home.

My father's summer furlough became distant as he returned to the army. By the time April arrived in 1975, North Vietnamese tanks had entered the capital as the South Vietnamese army retreated in defeat.

My father, a decorated officer, evaded capture behind enemy lines and returned home to the capital, Saigon, in time to evacuate his pregnant wife and three daughters to the airport. American marines guarding the airport check point insisted that my father discard his officer's uniform before they allowed him to join us at the end of the evacuation line.

While my father rummaged through abandoned luggage to find water bottles, a U.S. Chinook helicopter attempted to land and was blown up by surface-to-air missiles, showering blue and red flaming debris down upon us. Another Chinook landed, miraculously, and my mother, who was seven-months pregnant with her first son, lied to the marines about her advanced pregnancy so that our family could board the helicopter together. Once we were transported to the aircraft carrier, the U.S. *Hancock*, we took our place among hundreds of families occupying folding cots in the cavernous belly of this gigantic vessel, heading westward to Guam. After a rainy spring season in a refugee camp on this solitary island, our family was finally relocated by airplane to a marine base in southern California.

My childhood history provides a perspective on how the concept of self-care might seem superfluous to certain populations that experience a scarcity of food, shelter, and safety on a daily basis. I remember in high school having an argument with my father about his lack of warmth as a parent. Under my father's harsh criticism, I grew up like a trampled flower, straightening to reach the sun, only to get stepped on again. He compared my longing for connection to non-essential activities. "You wanted me to paint the walls while the house was on fire. I was keeping you alive."

What my father said sounds ironic in recent years considering that the continual striving for survival in today's modern society has created a movement of self-care. Most people might define self-care as devoting time to oneself to recharge or to promote wellness. Most of us long to yield to this desire. Where we might stumble in regards to self-care, however, is practicing it with frequency and without guilt. Throughout my life, I have felt the beckoning of water, and yet I have neglected its call while I pursued more urgent transitions in life, such as establishing work security after my divorce. In this chapter, I will share how to lean into discomfort to discover a self-care practice that can be consistent and guilt-free.

First Phase of Water (Unnatural)

As I emerged from my ocean swim this morning, the sensation of floating in the waves was imprinted on my body's sensory receptors as undulating crests and dips. I did not always feel comfortable in water. In Vietnam, when torrential rains flooded the narrow streets, I saw other kids play gleefully in waist-high water, while my mother sheltered us indoors. Once we arrived in the United States, our family was sponsored by a church community, and we were invited to pool parties. Bullying was a common occurrence in my childhood, and the rambunctious kids would taunt my inability to swim by dunking my head. Due to this negative imprinting from my childhood, I managed to avoid swimming until I reached high school, when a scheduling conflict inadvertently put me on the swim team for physical education class.

As a non-swimmer on the swim team, I had to figure out the sport on my own. My goggles leaked incessantly, and during the 6:30 practice every morning, my frustrated tears were disguised by the steam hovering low across the heated outdoor pool. I did not realize that I could swim straight down my lane by observing the black line painted on the bottom of the pool. Instead, my dominant right arm stroked harder than my left arm, and my right elbow would get bruised from hitting the plastic lane dividers floating on the surface. Worst of all, we had to begin races by jumping off the starting block, and I would lose my goggles and burn my eyes every time my head entered the water. I hope you are laughing with me now, because my introduction to swimming was a comedy of errors. It was so bad that when swim season ended, I gratefully retired my goggles.

In retrospect, why did I choose to remain on the swim team despite my distress? I leaned into discomfort because I related to my team's shared purpose. Learning to swim on my own, in the safety of our team practice, gave me confidence to explore the ocean later in life.

Second Phase of Water (Discovery)

Twenty years after high school, swimming resurfaced in my life, and it was the first time I considered it as self-care. At that stage in my life, I experienced a mysterious illness that put me on the medical merry-go-round. After a series of pulmonary function tests and skin allergy tests to diagnose a violent cough, my physician told me, "Your lab results are normal. Here's an antidepressant to help you cope with your symptoms." Ugh, taking even the smallest dose of that drug fogged my brain and made me feel disconnected, while my body continued to suffer.

After spending months on the couch, eating through the night because my condition disrupted my sleep and I could not control my bladder, I gained 40 pounds. I finally had enough when winter arrived, and I could not fit into my snow clothes. No one wants to buy new snow clothes that get worn only one season each year. Now motivated to improve my nutrition and clear blocked emotions, I decided to join a fitness club to rescue myself from this illusive illness for which I had received no diagnosis and no treatment. The only movement I could tolerate at that time was to float in the pool. It was an improvement over coughing on the couch.

At the fitness club, the first time I tried to swim a full length of the lap pool, I barely reached the other end; my high school swimming skills had regressed. Perhaps I might have quit, but a course catalogue from the recreation department arrived in my mailbox, and it offered scuba diving. To qualify for class, students had to be able to swim eight lengths of the pool, or four laps, for a total of 200 yards. Fascinated by the novelty of diving, I practiced until I could swim four laps without stopping. This small accomplishment cracked my self-limiting beliefs and brought me back to life. Next, I wanted to challenge myself to reach a bigger goal, to swim a mile, which I estimated as 1800 yards, 36 laps, or 72 times across the pool! When I met this goal, I wrote down my time and saved it as a personal best! By the time scuba diving class began, I was able to jump into the pool and swim the prerequisite four laps with ease. After this milestone, I left my mystery illness and its violent cough far behind.

Why did I embrace my discomfort of swimming laps by choosing an audacious goal such as scuba diving? I selected a milestone that was several skill levels above my current aptitude because I had no expectation of accomplishing that bold achievement. Any additional lap I was able to swim counted as a small win toward that epic finish, so the additional benefit of aiming for an ambitious goal was that it took pressure off the small, slow progress I made daily.

Third Phase of Water (Drought)

When the Great Recession hit in 2008, my husband moved to Europe for work, and our separation led to divorce. While raising two teenagers, I decided to enroll in nursing school so that I could return to my former profession in the medical device industry. I entered the traditional health system by completing a cardiovascular program at a nursing college. After becoming a Registered Cardiovascular Specialist, I assisted physicians in implanting medical devices in elite heart centers throughout the United States. In this environment, I saw that medical facilities treated patient symptoms with synthetic medications and invasive interventions, but these patients did not achieve whole health.

During these years of demanding travel and stressful patient cases, my only opportunities to swim were stolen moments between hotels and hospitals. Through daily exposure to many toxins from my work environment, such as jet fuel, food chemicals, and x-ray radiation, I experienced a painful jaw inflammation that had to be treated with antibiotics to prevent a dangerous systemic infection.

Being sick felt like déjà vu. This time, while doing internal healing work, I also devoted myself to understanding how environmental stressors had made me sick. I trained in complementary and alternative health practices and became certified as a Therapeutic Pain Specialist and a Clinical Nutritionist. These skills allowed me to assess external threats, such as food allergies, toxins, chemicals, metals, and scars, which disrupt the balance of our nervous system. By supporting the body's immune response, I could address nutritional deficiencies, which in turn, calm our fight or flight reactions, allowing our body to heal naturally. In my journey to understand our body's healing pathways, I was blessed to work with patients who leaned into discomfort while allowing their experience of illness to transform them physically, emotionally, and spiritually.

After leaving the hospital system, I launched my natural health clinic. The pandemic of 2020 caused my county to act as the first governing agency in the United States to order shelter-in-place. As a healthcare practitioner, my work was essential to supporting my clients' innate immunity. At first, I sprang into action, making sure that I knew the most current protocols for managing enveloped viruses. After the first month, being separated from my children while experiencing the lack of quarantine resources, my stress spiraled out of control. The community pool five minutes from my clinic was closed, so I did not cope well. Working late into the night, snacking to stay awake, I was not the role model for natural health I aspired for others. Two months later, my daughter came home to graduate from college through a virtual commencement. Having her presence brought back a semblance of normalcy, and she inspired me to go on a quest for the ocean.

Fourth Phase of Water (Integration)

Usually, the scenic drive over the Santa Cruz Mountains would take about fifty minutes, but the quarantine reduced traffic to a 35-minute trip. We arrived on the northern coast of California with sandy beaches framed by bluffs and rocks. I walked into the cold water, and it quenched my dry soul. Like a voluptuous woman, the ocean was full at high tide, her waves teased me when I got in, pulling me in different directions until I chased her into the deep. From that day, I began swimming in the ocean almost daily. Waking up at sunrise, driving over the mountains in fog and drizzle, not knowing if the coast would be overcast or sunny when I reached it. My swim adventure realigned my biology and set my priorities straight. When I start my day with this epic ritual of self-care, I no longer worry about what I cannot finish by the end of the day. Being in the big ocean assures me that the divine design will outlive my to-do list.

Inspired by the gifts of the ocean, I discovered how to share stories about the movement of water to connect people to my health practice. In addition to my previous clinical skills, I now also advocate for the benefits of cold-water therapy to help boost the immune system, increase blood circulation, heighten feel-good endorphins, reduce stress hormones, and stimulate metabolism for weight loss. The most profound lesson I discovered is that by tending to my self-care first, the business of living takes care of itself!

Lean into discomfort

Everything worth doing is on the other side.

A fatal flaw in our traditional practice of self-care is to seek comfort. We long to be sheltered from life's demands. Yet, clearing away stress through relaxation creates a void which attracts more stressors our way.

Have you ever left yoga or meditation practice, only to encounter traffic testing you on the way home? The transient nature of relaxation is why I seldom embrace comfort for my self-care practice.

Why is our brain wired to keep us in our comfort zone? Our brain receives information from our past experiences and from our current environment, through our sense of touch, smell, hearing, vision, and taste. The amygdala, which are special clusters of neurons in our brain, process this information as threats. Any disruption to our body's ability to keep homeostasis, or functional balance, is relayed to our nervous system and re-assessed by our brain. Our survival instinct depends on our brain to keep us safe by avoiding risks. Once our brain has been optimized for comfort, however, it becomes easily unsettled by any sign of stress.

What happens when we disrupt the traditional practice of self-care by embracing discomfort? When we engage in good stress, known as eustress, we feel the rush of adrenalin, the quickening of our heartbeat, the flush of nervous energy, all without dread. Remember the thrill of a carnival ride, the butterflies of a first date, the nervous performance of a public speech? When we raise the benchmark on how much internal *eustress* we can thrive on, we increase the threshold on how much external *distress* our body can handle. Did you achieve a personal best in your workout? This salient victory over eustress places our ubiquitous distress into better perspective. Even when we fall short of reaching goals, our choice to engage stress helps us build resilience while facing challenges.

The following framework has helped me to discover a self-care practice that is irresistible in spite of the challenge of maintaining it consistently and guilt-free:

- **What is your WHY?** At the core of your being, what allows you to experience joy? This internal motivation creates a compelling emotional connection which increases our resilience in overcoming obstacles that prevent us from tending to our self-care. Hint: What values would your family and friends say typically shape your behavior? I value freedom above all personal assets. I love walking into the ocean and allowing its gentle swells and currents to lift and carry me. When I am guided safely by nature, the act of swimming is an expression of my divine freedom.

1. **How do you serve others?** Examine your values to understand where pride in your work intersects with duty to others. This external

motivation allows you to express your unique skills and talents to grow your impact. Hint: The time spent on your self-care makes you a better partner, coach, or mentor to others. If you are a manual therapist, for example, getting frequent massages allows you to keep innovating your treatment technique. Swimming keeps me in good physical condition to be a credible health advocate, and the analogies I draw from the ocean help me to explain health concepts through more relatable stories.

2. **If you fail in all other aspects of your life, would this singular activity allow you to rebuild a new endeavor?** If you had to peddle your self-care skills, would someone pay to learn from you? Having confidence in your ability to monetize your skills allows you to devote time to seek your pleasure while reducing the pressure of diverting time and money from your "real work." Hint: when you speak about your self-care or post on social media, do people engage with your message and ask for more? For example, attending a stage show for self-care allows you to coach vocal skills to your voice students. To amplify my clinical work, I created a five-day retreat to immerse women in ocean swimming and nutritional therapy to empower their health transformation.

3. **Does your self-care help you thrive under stress?** This is the concept behind being anti-fragile, that embracing eustress will condition our autonomic nervous system not just to resist, but to thrive under distress. Hint: Are you engaging in daring feats which energize routine activities? To add a touch of daring to your routine, just take your activity outside. Walking on a nature trail adds elevation, temperature, and wildlife to an otherwise uninspiring treadmill session. When I begin my day with an ocean swim, I float in the space between endless sea and open sky. For the remainder of my day, all stressors are diminished by the shear grandeur of this opening experience.

Now, after having faced my own life challenges, if I were to talk with my father, I would tell him, "My house was on fire, but I learned skills to build a new one. My self-care kept me alive." I would love to hear how you are implementing this self-care framework as you lean into discomfort! I wish you tremendous success in creating a self-care ritual that will remain consistent and guilt-free. I invite you to come swim with me for more inspiration . . .

Kelsey Bassanini

Kelsey Bassanini, RCIS ACN TPS, is an open water swimmer who empowers women to conquer self-limiting beliefs in water, so they can transform naturally on land.

Kelsey earned her degree in Mechanical Engineering at Stanford University. She also graduated Summa Cum Laude from Lancaster General College of Nursing and Health Sciences. Kelsey worked as a registered cardiovascular specialist in elite hospitals all over the country. After observing patients suffering from unresolved pain and chronic medical conditions, she became certified as a therapeutic pain specialist and an applied clinical nutritionist.

In 15 years of working in both traditional and natural health, Kelsey experienced her own amazing healing journey through open water. She began taking women to swim in the ocean to show them that the cold and scary waves can be managed safely. When women learned how to adapt to the changing conditions in the ocean, they quickly transformed from a lost soul into an empowered creator. Guided by Kelsey, women walk into the waves feeling fragile and anxious, and they return to shore feeling elated and victorious that they have conquered their self-limiting beliefs!

After submitting this chapter for publication, Kelsey was deployed by the State of California as an emergency medical responder to train health providers being sent into hot zones to care for patients infected with COVID-19. While enhancing their clinical proficiency, Kelsey also shared with these frontline health workers essential self-care practices to upgrade their immune system through breathwork, energy tuning, wholesome nutrition, and healing touch.

Name: Kelsey Bassanini, RCIS ACN TPS
Email Address: **kelsey@KelseyBassanini.com**
Phone Number:415-666-6213
Website: **www.KelseyBassanini.com**
Facebook page: **https://www.facebook.com/kelsey.bassanini.rcis**
LinkedIn Page: **linkedin.com/in/kelseybassanini**

FROM MUD TO LOTUS
BY ANN JONAS

"Both suffering and happiness are of an organic nature,
which means they are both transitory; they are always
changing. The flower, when it wilts, becomes the compost.
The compost can help grow a flower again. Happiness
is also organic and impermanent by nature."
–Thich Nhat Hanh

NO MUD, NO LOTUS

Over the last two decades, I have navigated the energy of the lotus, physically on my body, throughout my business life, and in my spiritual message. In 2003, my journey with the lotus flower came through a stained-glass window, in the sacred space of a dear friend. I describe it as a God moment since I was asking for an idea for a tattoo that would have a spiritual meaning for me. This image is what birthed my first business as a bodyworker and birth doula, The Lotus Touch. On July 22, 2005, my life dramatically changed with the death of my mother. Then in 2014, a year after becoming a single mother, I followed a passion to become a life coach and I evolved my next business into The Lotus Coach. This part of my journey led me to developing my first workshop: "Moving from Horrendous to Heroic: The Seven Strategies for a Conscious Life." Another shift occurred when I realized that my message was reflective of a more inclusive process of evolution. I found my way to the final iteration, incorporating wholeness, seeing as the cycles we journey are not linear but circular or spiraled. **What I developed was, "The Lotus Path: The Great Circling. No Mud, No Lotus." In 2019, I held my first weekend retreat "Got Gratitude," and was inspired to make retreats a regular part of my offering.**

I have been encouraged many times to write my story. I am excited and honored to participate in this anthology that will help people empower themselves. I love that in this supportive platform, with my colleagues from multiple dimensions and approaches, we are sharing our own individual quality of offering.

Through the decades of holding space, for birth through doula work and as a bodyworker, **I know the beautiful mess that this life is as we come home, to connect presence with self.** As I have found my own ground and stability from the depth of the challenges, to meet and accept my own path, I know how to hold others where they are. Encouraging and being a true witness and guide as I have learned to be for myself. **My passion and desire is to serve human beings in the unveiling of the higher self and allowing the spirit to bring abundant happiness and love.**

What I am presenting here is the story of how I have looked at my life and recognized it as a metaphor for the lotus' expression from the mud. I have reflected on how I navigated through experiences that most people consider traumatic and challenging. **I discovered that there was a calm somewhere deep inside me that allowed me to be empowered by the desire to move through these experiences and learn what they want to show and teach me, pulling me through the muck.** The way of seeing my life stories as important, relevant, and that everything happens for a reason, have been how I celebrated that I was offering the perspective of how we all have mud; it doesn't matter what kind, **we may choose to see our life as a journey of evolution or not.**

When we are willing to look at life though this approach, we stand on the path and we begin to recognize that our life is the product of our responses and reactions. Jack Canfield speaks of the success formula for life being $E + R = O$. In essence, the **Events/Experiences** in our life are the foundation and then we add the **Reactions/ Responses** and that equates to the **Outcome**. How we see ourselves and our stories is not based on what happened, but how we navigated and dealt with it. That is truly the story we are telling.

I believe that everything happens for a reason. My parents were divorced when I was 11. The day that profoundly impacted my life, occurred 25 years later. My father, after a life of bi-polar shifts and suicide attempts, came to my mother's home, the one I grew up in, removed a gun from a paper bag, shot her twice and left her for dead. This experience was a significant turning point in my life and in the lives of many others.

My mother's death, an experience that many have heard me talk about, was a launching pad for a new direction in my life, an evolution of my spiritual growth. In 2013, eight years after my mother died, my life direction shifted again when my spouse, and other mom to our daughter, transitioned, after a four-year journey with Melanoma. Each of these experiences and many others influenced how my life shifted, what was released and what was birthed anew.

How is it that I have been able to navigate these experiences and not feel bitter? Well, I have had all of the emotions that one would assume would come with having your mother murdered by your father and then having your spouse die from cancer, leaving you as a single mother. I have felt frustration, anger, disbelief, immense grief, and powerlessness, but I was also curious. It was not from a place of "Why is this happening?" but "How is this going to teach me about life, about myself?" **As I look back over my life, what I have come to learn and put into words, is that I have somehow always known that things happen FOR me and not TO me.**

As I think back over the last 15 years and how my life has changed, what I have learned about myself and the perspective that I have on life, **I know that our experiences through the mud will help us to flower and blossom.** In addition, I have realized through my life journey that operating from a conscious perspective includes some basic principles or strategies and this is how I have come to daily navigate the things that life throws at me.

Trust/Faith

"If prayer is you talking to God, then intuition is God talking to you."
—*Wayne Dyer*

It all starts with trusting that everything you are experiencing is what you need to be going through in order to grow and evolve. This means trusting that all is serving in the greater good of your unfolding life. Trusting that there is a higher power at work, a larger energy.

This leads to faith. Here is where I want to talk about the word God. As Alan Watts says, "You cannot get wet from the word water." Language is powerful and often how we connect with words is different, but when we move beyond the word and into the true meaning, then you can call it whatever you want It, the word, becomes a shared understanding of the essence of how you feel when you say it. I don't care what you want to call it: Goddess, Universe, Energy, Mystery, Divine, Spirit, Love. Just decide that you believe it to exist and that it is The Everything. God is light and God is love. From this knowledge of and belief in a Higher Power grows faith. This faith creates a relationship, one where you believe there is some form of communication through reading holy writings, attending services, saying blessings over meals, praying for help/assistance for self or others, chanting, and meditating.

When you decide that you have faith and you trust in a greater power, then you are walking through life with this energy by your side; you feel more secure in your choices, or at least, you trust that it is meant to be. There is a story in the footprints poem where the man is walking in the sand and notices that in most of his life there are two sets of foot prints yet when life is hardest there are only one, and he asks God, "Where were you then?" The response is, "I was carrying you." Trust the greater power to carry you, especially during those hard and challenging times... you are never alone.

2) Acceptance

"Yesterday is history, tomorrow is a mystery, today is
a gift of God, which is why we call it the present."
—*Bil Keane, American Cartoonist*

We receive all kinds of gifts in a lifetime and some come in very ugly packaging. It is through acceptance that we allow the experiences in our lives to be teachers. It is a choice to let go of our attachment to a story and just be present with what has shown up, not trying to dismiss or deny. Understandably it is easy to accept when the things that come through make sense and we are grateful that we have had this experience. What about when you do not want to accept? This is where the deeper work comes. Choosing to accept things we do not like, such as an illness or a loss, is asking us to recognize that the hard stuff, while it is not fun, is necessary for our true evolution. How do you accept something that you do not want in your life? One step at a time, one breath at a time, one moment at a time. From that space we can look inward for how this experience is necessary for us to truly learn about ourselves and the reason that we are here at this time.

"Acceptance is neither resignation nor powerlessness but an opening of the way for the next right actions." *--Tosha Silver, Author*

3) Personal growth

"Desire is the starting point of all achievement."
—Napoleon Hill, Author

We are not the bodies that came through our mother's birth canal, we have grown and evolved each day since. Acknowledging that our life is a journey invites us to step fully into understanding that we must be willing to go through the hard stuff, the "missteps," "mess-ups," the falls, and the mistakes and keep going. **When we decide that this is a personal growth journey, then we keep showing up for the next adventure.**

"The path isn't a straight line; it's a spiral. You continually come back to things you thought you understood and see deeper truths."
—Barry H. Gillespie, Author

4) Community

"Alone, we can do so little; together, we can do so much"
—Helen Keller

In the animal kingdom, it has been determined that animals must live in community, the individual will not survive alone. This is an innate knowing. As humans, we believe that we can choose isolation, it has the illusion of safety through control. When in truth, the layers of how we show up get peeled away when we are connected to and supported by a community of like-minded and supportive members. Yes, it makes sense that a challenging childhood or even adulthood can leave the experience of community feeling damaging or lack luster. Therefore, in the vein of leading a conscious life and feeling supported to navigate challenges, it would behoove us to see that community is beneficial and necessary.

"We have all known the long loneliness and we have learned that the only solution is love and that love comes with community." --*Dorothy Day, American Journalist*

5) Honesty with self and others

"Honesty and transparency make you vulnerable.
Be honest and transparent anyway."
—Mother Teresa

Many of us have heard the saying that honesty builds character and building character with ourselves might be one of the hardest tasks of all. Of course, we know when we are not being honest and it all comes back to the choices we make. We can either choose to show up with authenticity or get lost in our lies and our stories. *The reality is that how we show up and what we do always matters. We learn to stay no matter what is happening. We are learning to love ourselves as we are.*

6) Self-love

*"Every one of us needs to show how much we care for
each other and, in the process, care for ourselves."*
—Diana, Princess of Wales

We are told to put the oxygen mask on ourselves first, this is how we can help others. This is a process of unfolding and holding ourselves with compassion and it is a part of navigating a conscious life.

*"Owning our story and loving ourselves through that
process is the bravest thing that we'll ever do."*
—Brené Brown

7) Gratitude

*"Gratitude makes sense of our past, brings peace
for today and creates a vision for tomorrow."*
—Melody Beattie

We are invited to see every moment as an opportunity to be thankful for simply being alive, sometimes that is all we can do. Have gratitude for the simple, the mundane, the great and the challenging. It is in gratitude that we will see at least a sliver of light, just enough to pierce the veil of pain. If we are in a place of light, then we are building the energy toward the next place of growth. **When we have gratitude, we are willing to be more gracious and accepting.**

In conclusion, life is a journey and we are all here to learn.

*"We are not human beings having a spiritual experience;
we are spiritual beings having a human experience."*
—Pierre Teilhard de Chardin

Through decades of supporting others through this work I have learned the following: When we align to exist as a human being for the greater purpose of growth as a spiritual being, than I believe we take some of the pressure off and allow ourselves to be in the playground of life on planet Earth. This helps us go from the mud experience in life to full blossom as a beautiful lotus flower.

I miss my mother's physical presence and I am sorry that my daughter never met her grandparents. I miss my partner and I know my daughter does too, but I trust the way my life has and will continue to unfold. I trust the process of life, the connections and the disconnections, and I am always grateful to be able to share my message.

Our lives are made up of one step at a time, one choice at a time. These choices are dependent on our willingness to grow and personal presence. It is a unique path for each person, it is sacred and individual.

It is my wish that you will come away from this chapter with the belief that you are capable of moving from the mud in your life to the lotus when you choose to embrace these principles.

Ann Jonas

Ann Jonas, Transformational Coach, is passionate about helping and supporting others to become more of who they truly are. She approaches her work from a holistic, intuitive, spiritual perspective with decades of experience as a bodyworker and birth doula. Today, her most powerful gift is being a personal life coach, writer, speaker, and workshop facilitator.

Ann knows the beautiful mess that this life is as we move through the process of coming home to connection and presence with self. She helps those who feel disconnected from themselves, or not in alignment with their inner knowing, to feel more aware of who they are so they can have a deeper understanding of how they see themselves and their stories. They feel more relaxed and connected to their whole self as well as their families and communities.

The Lotus Path is made of our own life and gifts that are calling to come forth. As Ann found her ground and stability from the depth of her challenges, she met and accepted her own path and she knows how to hold others where they are, encouraging and being a true witness and guide, as she has learned to be those things for herself. Ann's passion and desire are to serve human beings in the unveiling of the higher self and allow the spirit to bring abundant happiness and love.

misslotus@comcast.net

415-312-6416

www.thelotuspath.love

https://www.facebook.com/pg/annthelotuspath/posts

https://www.linkedin.com/in/ann-jonas-463a669

https://www.youtube.com/
playlist?list=PLx8vTVjMGi88NDnXkOqb33yx-ZAnGMdRv

PART THREE: INFORMED GUIDANCE

TRUSTING THE SELF

SEQUESTERED INTO SELF-LOVE
BY AERIOL ASCHER

When my guides told me 20 years ago that I was supposed to talk about self-love I did not really understand the message. In fact, I remember at one point thinking that meant that I would never be in a relationship until I achieved a certain state of "self-love." Being a tenacious creature and not really wanting to be alone, I decided to marry myself. I bought a ring and everything! I held a little symbolic ceremony to pledge my love to my higher self, putting that relationship before any other.

I would get to a place where I would think I had accepted the message, and then I would forget. I mean like, really forget. I let my weight get out of control at one point and I remember not even caring! I was busy working on other parts of my life and did not have the bandwidth to focus on that part, or so I thought.

After closing my holistic healing center, I was a mess. My ego was bruised from having to let go of my seeming success, I was broke, I was stressed, and my body was holding a ton of inflammation. The couple years after that got even more stressful on a personal level when I lost my three aging dogs who had been my primary support and family system for the last 18 to 20 years.

After serving so many others for the past 30 years of my adult life, I reluctantly got to work on my self on an even deeper level. I got more disciplined with myself in my meditation and journaling practices, which I'd been doing but not consistently, and I participated in some group self-mastery energy classes to build community on that level.

I worked on my self-care. I felt better, I called back my power, and was doing good. I got even more diligent with my own energetic healing practice. My daily life became much slower than I was accustomed, but I was comfortable. Then, just when I thought I was at the end of my journey into self . . . a worldwide pandemic in 2020 interrupted the entire year of traveling and speaking that I was projecting for myself for the upcoming year.

I shifted the focus of the "Healing Body Mind and Soul Network" podcast to having self-care experts share their take on the subject. I used my network as a platform to host these guests and to help get self-care support to people all over the world who needed it. I just began interviewing every healing practitioner, spiritual teacher, and coach I came across in order to get as many points of view as possible. Do you want to know what I discovered?

My guides were right all along. They have never steered me wrong. As long as I tuned in and listened to them, I'd always had their support and guidance. The healing modalities, the mystical concepts, the emotional charges, and the psychic impressions that led me to do my work in the world has really paid off. I learned so much from interviewing experts in related empowerment and wellness fields. What I know is that with science and quantum physics finally reaching the point that we are learning about the power of the bio-energetic field, the subtle energies of the Earth, the balance of the left and right hemispheres of the brain, the power of our minds, and the power of our hearts, it is a wonderful and magical time to be alive on the planet. We have the opportunity to witness huge advancements in technology and transitions in humanity.

What do these advancements have to do with self-love? The more you love yourself, the better you'll take care of your whole self. This includes your physical, emotional, mental, and spiritual well-being. On an energetic level, each of these areas affect the space you reside in (your physical body as well as your environment), the people around you, and ultimately the world or reality that you inhabit. Your level of self-love impacts your health, longevity, emotional self-esteem, self-confidence, and success.

When you love yourself, you make yourself your number one priority. You deserve nothing less than your own full attention.

Try these strategies to cultivate greater self-love

1. **Document your wins in life.** It's easy to get in a funk or to focus on failures. Try doing the opposite for a month and see what happens! Write down all the great things that happen. Collect a list of all your greatest achievements. Keep a living biography of your greatness in a document. It can be composed of compliments people gave you, testimonials clients sent, or achievements. One of the easiest ways to remember your victories is to catalogue them in this fashion. You can take this a step further and create a scrapbook of your achievements for you to look at when you need a pick me up. I had a humbling experience with this upon closing my center and downsizing my practice. I pasted all the social media comments, testimonials, press releases, and reviews. I was stunned to compile a 10,000-word document validating my life's work. It still brings me to tears each time I open that document on my computer.

2. **Forgive yourself.** Every person has a past. I *highly suggest you keep the learnings and release the rest.* Every person has made a few mistakes, file away the wisdom and alter your behavior in the future. Learn from your mistakes, but don't hold on to the energy or beat yourself up with them. I often suggest the practice of energetic healing techniques like Ho'o Pono-Pono, a technique that Hawaiian Shaman would use to set the energy right after a discrepancy or upset. It is intended to set free the energy charge so that it does not live inside the person as a resentment and fester into a disease in the physical body. While this technique is often used to correct perceived wrongs done upon us by a perpetrator, it can be applied to the self with great success.

3. **Pursue what you need rather than what you want.** Anyone who has ever listened to the Rolling Stones is familiar with this concept. Mick Jager, while one may question his own motivations, had it right. "You can't always get what you want, but if you try sometimes, you may find you get what you need." While I am not sure where Mick stands on this, I know that taking care of one's primary needs are essential. Perhaps the difficulty in interoperation here lies in determining what is truly essential? Never before have more people been tested in this area than

during shelter-in-place orders during a global pandemic. Satisfying your own primary needs is a prime example of self-love.

4. **Take care of your body.** This is a complicated one. However, does it need to be? I think the complicated part is figuring out what is best for yourself as an individual. For me, even though I had gained some weight, my self-esteem was much higher and I had lots of perceived energy because I was in some exciting situations. I felt it was important to accept where I was at and be grateful for my circumstances. It was finally the winning combination of my body telling me it was ready to shed the weight and the radical change in lifestyle due to the pandemic's social restrictions that led me to do some nutritional cleansing and try out a new line of products. My already downsized healing practice came to a screeching halt and, having no one-on-one client consultations during long periods of shelter-in-place, I suddenly no longer required the essential oils I was purchasing to serve other people. My guides nudged me to switch my energy to the nutritional cleansing products offered by a different product line than I had used before. I trusted the guides so I jumped in. Within two days I was convinced my body had been starved for nutrition and that flooding it with these products was like turning on a faucet of healing grace. I kept asking my sponsor if it was normal to start tingling all over with these cleansing products? I felt as if scrubbing bubbles were inside helping me let go of toxins. (Sounds a little like our Ho'o Pono-Pono that we mentioned earlier, doesn't it?) At the time of writing this chapter, I am about halfway through a huge weight loss goal that has miraculously resulted in weight dropping off my frame.

5. **Appreciate your own interests and uniqueness.** When I was little I had the unusual experience of going to a dozen or more schools. I became aware that I had a talent for re-inventing myself with better social strategies to try to fit in to new groups, new schools, and new circumstances, sometime multiple times a year, while I was in my formative years. I had to start from scratch with new peers over and over again and developed a certain level of tolerance to that social stressor in my life. I became a shapeshifter. I've shared before that I was labeled "over-sensitive" and that I have a tendency to be "a lot" of energy for other sensitive people. I have a "strong presence" because I developed a very strong sense of self due to my upbringing and subsequently my studies of theatre arts, mysticism, metaphysics, and holistic arts. Socially, however, I would often squelch my energy or opinion so as not to appear "bossy" or like a "know-it-all." When I was young I

would sometimes completely try to hide my subtle sensitivities or to "dumb down" myself so people (usually attractive men I had nothing in common with) would like me or accept me. However, the most valuable parts of me are some of those parts that show up uniquely in me. From the bottom of my heart, I encourage you to embrace the rich mixture of qualities that make you who you are!

6. **Practice extreme gratitude.** There is a reason that every spiritual teacher from every tradition has some take on this. Practicing gratitude changes the energy in your brain, your heart, and your body. By practicing gratitude, you put yourself into a divine energetic flow that exponentially improves your situation and surroundings. Be grateful for your body, your mind, and your uniqueness. Be grateful for napkins, be grateful for shoes, be grateful for every single thing in your life. Your life is better than you think. You are better than you think. Be grateful, and feel yourself shift into a state of graceful flow.

7. **Be as kind to yourself as you would be to anyone else.** If you had a tape recorder tracking what you tell yourself in your head each day, what would it be like to listen to that tape? Would it be a wicked tale of intrigue and suspense under the wrath of an evil ruler, or would it be a benevolent narrator recounting an enchanted dream? You know the choice is yours, right? Then why is it so easy for us to extend kindness, time, love, devotion, attention to others, and not to ourselves? To put it really bluntly, to be kinder to others than you are to yourself is just showing everyone, including yourself, that you don't respect yourself. This can be a tough pill to swallow if you are at the other end of this equation. The starting point? If this book is in your hand you have already started. Be kind and understanding to yourself.

Self-love as part of your dedicated self-care practice is an essential part of your personal self-development. Your primary relationship is with the Self. For me, it manifested as giving myself freedom to create, being of service to the world, and cultivating a deep relationship with my higher self so that I can raise my frequency and commune with my angels, masters, and guides. Self-love may very well manifest differently for you. It is your personal responsibility to discover that for yourself. Until you do, your success and happiness in this lifetime are seriously at risk.

Self-love is a skill that can be developed, a muscle that can be flexed. But like your muscles respond to lifting weight, the effect of building a strong sense of self-love does not happen overnight, but rather cumulatively with consistent effort over time. Self-love is the end result of an effective set of daily habits. Set aside some time each day to build your self-esteem and self-love by embracing practices that feed your soul. By choosing to enrich and care for yourself first, your life will be infinitely richer.

To support you in your own self-healing you can check out some of the self-healing and mindfulness meditation tools always available at my website: **https://aeriolascher.com/free-self-healing**. But I also wanted to offer you a very special download of my free e-book. It is my chapter from the international best-seller *The Animal Legacies* entitled: "The Force of Nature." The reason I am sharing this particular story is because it is really about self-awareness, self-healing, and most of all, LOVE. It is my personal heart-healing story of how I had to follow my own intuition, inner-voice, and dream-guidance to heal myself from the tremendous grief and trauma caused by the loss of my dog Easter and open my heart to love. Even if you are not an animal lover, it is my hope that you will find some truth for yourself in reading my story. I hope that you are inspired to heal and to delve deeply into your own soul's journey, awakening, and self-healing. Get your FREE download at: **https://aeriolascher.com/free-love/**

Aeriol Ascher

Aeriol Ascher, MsD. is an internationally best-selling author, metaphysical healing master, and speaker success coach from San Jose, CA. She is the producer and host of the Healing Body Mind and Soul Podcast and the founder of the **bodymindsoul.tv** and media network. It is Aeriol's personal mission to raise the consciousness of the planet one soul at a time and she believes that by leading, producing, and publishing holistic media and programs that educate, uplift, and inspire, she is doing her part. She must be doing something right because her video series *Self-Care* under quarantine earned her two 2020 Communicator Awards of Distinction from the Academy of Interactive Visual Arts.

As a holistic educator, Aeriol empowers her clients with tools to increase body awareness, hone intuition, and connect to their highest self so they can confidently and authentically navigate their personal and professional lives. She has a passion for facilitating group healing experiences that awaken self-awareness, inspire growth, and create a safe and sacred learning environment for spiritual awakening, personal empowerment, and fun.

As a women's empowerment leader, Aeriol has a passion for guiding heart-centered entrepreneurs, practitioners, educators, and coaches to show up, speak up, and stand out so they can embrace their authentic and soul-aligned success. Aeriol offers them strategic guidance, speaker training, best-selling book publishing projects, public speaking events, and visibility opportunities on the "Healing Body Mind and Soul" podcast and the **bodymindsoul.tv** and media network, as well as affiliate platforms, including the RHG Media Network and VoiceAmerica TV Network.

Whether you are in need of self-care support, or you are a healer on a mission (or both!), you will want to lean in and join the bodymindsoul .tv and media network. For more information please reach out to Aeriol at: **AeriolAscher.com**

https://www.facebook.com/Aeriol
https://www.facebook.com/AskAeriol
https://www.facebook.com/reikiangelacademy
https://www.instagram.com/askaeriol/
https://youtube.com/c/HealingBodyMindandSoulNetwork
https://www.linkedin.com/in/aeriolascher/

A QUESTION OF BALANCE
BY AIMEE LYNDON-ADAMS

Never before in the history of the planet has humanity been given such a powerful opportunity to evaluate how we are living our lives.

Yes, overnight, the global pandemic brought the world to stillness. No longer able to live the lives we had been living, each one of us were given a chance to re-examine how we spend our time and money. While some of us responded to the needs of our communities and found ourselves exhausted from working harder than ever, others watched their work and livelihoods disappear at the drop of a hat. While it is very tempting to feel victimized by circumstances, in truth, we created this opportunity for a reset because we knew humanity needed to change its behavior: we knew we had to change.

More and more people are discovering what they have been missing. It doesn't matter how much you love your work, too much work throws you out of balance. Distractions rob you of your creative time. Too much doing often leads to resentment and exhaustion, it deprives you of your time to simply be, and, when our focus is only external, we neglect the wisdom and whispers of the soul.

> *I used to work as an executive in a Fortune 500 company based in San Francisco, putting in the typical 12 to 14 hour-day. One day, at 7 pm, as I was sitting at my computer, I heard a loud voice in my head, "Go home now!" it said. I answered, "I will in a minute – just let me finish this memo." Again, the voice said, even more strongly this time, "Go home NOW!" "I will, I will – just let me finish this up!" I begged. And, then my back went out . . .*

Many of us would agree that relationships are the most important aspect of a well-lived life and yet, investment in our friendships are often the first thing to go when we stuff our lives with busyness. Similarly, we might say our intimate partnership and our families are the priority, but again, are your actions in alignment with that belief? And, for many of us, it's the relationships with ourselves that suffer the most – would you agree?

> *After three successful divorces, I got to own that I was prioritizing my work over my love life! Never again, I promised, when I met my beloved 15 years ago. And you know what? I made and kept a set of boundaries that have allowed my relationship to blossom and flourish over all these years. It's not what you say is important, but what you do to demonstrate that you mean it.*

Have you taken the time to rethink how you are living your life? What have you learned? What do you want to do differently? Do you believe that you deserve to live a balanced life that respects your natural rhythms, that allows you the time for renewal, one that allows you to explore your curiosity, experience the richness of relationship, the beauty of this planet, and the divinity of your soul?

As a divine being, given the amazing gift of a human physical body and life on this exquisite planet, your primary responsibility must be to yourself. Whether you are a boss, an employee, an entrepreneur, a mother, a wife, or a caretaker, you are the commodity! If you don't take care of yourself, you cannot truly be there for others in your life – however much you might want to be! And that sets you up to be disappointed in yourself which further depletes you.

On the other hand, when you give from your energetic fullness or your energetic overflow, you always give your best to others.

Self-care technique: fill and refill yourself

Fill yourself up energetically before giving to others and after giving, refill yourself. That way, you are always giving from a place of fullness versus depletion.

So, what fills you up?

For me, it's my heart-centered grounding and centering process, yoga nidra, art journaling, playing with a pet, connecting with my spirit guides, meditation, time in nature, gentle movement like hatha yoga, savoring a cup of tea in a bone china teacup, making love with my beloved, Epsom salt baths, time alone, and letting go of doing and relaxing into being.

What about you? Are you in touch with what fulfills you? Do you know the difference between a need and a want? A need is something without which you do not function well – like getting enough sleep, being physically touched, spending quality alone time, etc. A want is something you prefer or something you might like to have.

I grew up believing that my own needs were unimportant, unobtainable and that it was safer to have no needs to avoid disappointment. Like many of us who don't believe their needs can be met, I went after my wants/desires instead, only to discover that my wants will never fill the hole left by my unmet needs.

The truth is that almost everyone I meet is exhausted: physically, mentally, emotionally and some, even spiritually! Yes, it can be exhausting to worry about your purpose and destiny, your contribution in the world, making a difference with your life.

Self-care technique: inventory your needs

The following list of needs freely shared by the Center for Non-Violent Communication is neither exhaustive nor definitive. It is meant as a starting point that supports anyone who wishes to engage in the process of self-discovery and that facilitates greater understanding and connection between people.

https://www.cnvc.org/training/resource/needs-inventory

Once you have identified your needs, the next step is to figure out how to get them met. Some you will be able to fulfil by yourself, and once you understand that it is your responsibility to attend to your own needs, you will make it a priority. Other needs require the participation of your intimate partner and/or your family. First, make sure you have the full attention of the person you are addressing. This is essential. Next, ask *cleanly* for what you need. Asking cleanly means no guilt-tripping, no dragging up past behavior, no making anybody wrong. Explain *clearly* what it is that you want, what it would look like, how often, at what time, etc. Be precise! You must translate what you want into clear, actionable behavior – behavior that the person can understand, know he/she can succeed at. Be willing for him/her to say, "no." It's a request, not an order. And if he does say, "no" or "not at this time"–ask if you can circle back later, at a better time. Then think about who else could provide what you need and ask them. If you persist, you will succeed. And persistence is a demonstration of your own self-esteem and investment in your own self-care.

As we rethink how we live, I would like to put forward some provocative thoughts for your consideration.

> *As a child, I was very interested and skilled in drawing and painting. I proudly told my father that when I grew up, I wanted to be an artist. His reply shaped the first forty years of my life. "Oh, honey" he said, "Keep what you love to do as your hobby. Work is what you get paid to do – because you wouldn't do it unless they paid you." It took me many years to shake off this faulty programming. Over my time in corporate, the extended hours, artificial lighting, lengthy commutes and high stress levels, disconnected my body from its natural rhythms, and I started putting on weight. Arriving home at 8 pm, all I wanted was a glass of wine, or two, a meal and to go to sleep. I realized that it didn't matter how much money I was earning (and it was a lot) since I had no time to enjoy it!*

Human beings were never designed to be enslaved to their work or to money. I learned the hard way that corporate life is unfulfilling, while expecting or demanding that you be loyal to it, is not loyal to you. We've learned that our retirement savings can be wiped out overnight through "redistribution of wealth" tactics and, similarly, we can be cheated out of our own homes by the financial institutions we erroneously place our trust in.

Self-care stipulates that you place yourself carefully: where you can thrive not merely survive. Self-care ensures that you are seen and valued and not merely seen as an account number or a bank balance.

Now, I consider my work to be "high play." You see, I channel the wisdom and healing energy of 20 Ascended Master Guides through my hands and words. As their energy comes through me, I feel lit up like a Christmas tree. Every cell of my body is enlivened and I experience extreme mental clarity that is connected to and directed by my heart. I arrive at each session or event with excitement and anticipation. It is truly a joy to be of service to my community and I notice my creativity accelerating with new possibilities all of the time. Time literally stops still when I am working as I am totally present in the here and now, and in the flow of life.

Take a moment and think of your experiences of high play. Have you experienced time stopping still when you are doing something you love? Is it something that could be shared with others, something you could be remunerated for?

As you rethink how you want to live, can you imagine a life where you rested until you wanted to practice high play and then rested again when you wanted to? Can you imagine the impact of such a life on your being? Because so many of us are so exhausted, it may be hard to imagine.

Self-care technique: yoga nidra

This is not a hard sell! Yoga nidra simply involves lying down and listening to a guided meditation that rotates your awareness through the physical body, switching off the mind and allowing you to access levels of rest twice as deep as the deepest point of sleep. Practicing yoga nidra has changed the quality of my life and it can do the same for you too. A favorite site is www.DaringToRest.com

If the suggestion to rest until you want to play, and play until you want to rest, feels out of reach, here's another balance model to consider. Fifty percent of your time is spent on your own self-care and the other half is spent on taking care of others.

I made the point earlier that the most effective way of giving comes from giving from your energetic overflow – when you give from depletion, you are not giving anything of value.

Years ago, a colleague who suffered from fierce migraines told me a story about her child. She came to realize that reading to her child during a migraine caused the child to wonder if she had been naughty, as mommy sounded so angry. Instead, she decided to explain that mommy wasn't feeling well and was going to put on a favorite video for the child so she could lie down for a little while and would read to the child when she arose, feeling better.

If you tend to put your own needs on the back burner, you may feel resentful towards those that succeed in getting their needs met, or you may be feeling at a loss as to how to proceed in getting your own needs met.

First, you need to re-evaluate your values and your priorities. Is the way you are living your life making you happy? Do you really need all of the things you buy, or do you use shopping either as a distraction or as a substitute for getting your needs met? Can you envision living a simpler life in which you are doing what you love and are surrounded by the people you most love, and have time for? Can you imagine being well-rested?

What would you need to stop doing? What would you need to start doing? How many pointless things are you doing for no current, valid reason—just because you've always done them? What if you only did the things that bring you joy and found other solutions to handle the rest? If you have children, a job, a home and a partner, I understand that it will take more focus and determination, and yet, it can still be done. You've got to want it more than the status quo.

Working with either of these self-care models requires the courage to put yourself first. It may bring up feelings of low self-worth. Sometimes you may feel like you are taking two steps forward and one step backwards. Some days you may think it isn't worth it and want to go back to the old ways where you had no time to think or feel. However, on the days you succeed and get to express all of yourself, your innate gifts and talents, including your own unique imprint of your soul's essence can emerge. At that point, you will unquestionably know that a life lived in balance is worth it and so are you!

If you have enjoyed my chapter and found it thought provoking, I invite you to stay in touch by joining my mailing list. You will also receive a beautiful gift: "33 Ways to Raise Your Frequency." Just go to **www.AimeeLyndon-Adams.com**.

Aimée Lyndon-Adams

Aimée Lyndon-Adams is passionately committed to guiding those of you who are on the spiritual path to clear the imprinting, programming, and wounding that gets in the way of you living the life of your dreams, in the flow of abundance, experiencing dynamic health, enjoying true relationship intimacy, and fulfilling your own purpose.

If you are looking for a proven professional who can guide you in how to radically redesign your life, to break the habit of over-giving and over-working, and to learn how to raise your frequency into the fifth dimension, you've come to the right place.

With 30 years of experience working with amazing clients with similar worries and concerns, and guiding them to achieve remarkable success, my mission and commitment is to support extraordinary women of all races, religions, countries of origin, and sexual orientations, along with the men that support them, as I believe that it is the western woman that will change the world.

What sets me apart from other practitioners is that I share purpose with 20 ascended master guides and channel their love, wisdom, and healing energy through my words and hands.

Five things about me and my experience that might surprise and delight you and serve our work together are that I served as an executive in several Fortune 500 companies, specializing in sales and customer service, and with an International Training Company as a senior consultant and executive coach, my 20 ascended masters and I can see you at a soul level, I have overcome a life-threatening disease, and I have enjoyed a deeply intimate and harmonious relationship with my beloved for 15 years and counting.

My perspectives have been featured in WHF magazine, **https://www.wfhmag.net**

Sybil magazine **https://whattrulymatters.com/author/aimee/** and in my book, *Raise My Vibes: The Practical Path to Joy* **https://www.amazon.com/s?k=Raise+my+Vibes&i=stripbooks&ref=nb_sb_noss**

Aimee@AimeeLyndon-Adams.com
707-304-4962
www.AimeeLyndon-Adams.com
www.facebook.com/aimeelyndonadams
linkedin.com/in/ALyndonAdams

EVERYTHING IS ELECTRICITY
BY SUE WILHITE

Gasps and even some small screams erupted from the class during the high school chemistry lecture on thermodynamics. We had watched the teacher place a medium-sized beaker containing a white powder on the tall end of a block of wood in front of him. He talked about chemical bonds, and about the energy gained and lost as bonds changed. As he spoke, he slowly poured more white powder in the beaker. He finished his little talk by saying, ". . . and when you've loosened all the bonds, and released all the energy, you end up with this!" He hefted the beaker into the air—and the block of wood came with it! They had frozen together! It was so startling and unexpected that we all reacted audibly as he had intended. (The powders he'd mixed were similar to those instant hand warmer packets, only instant freeze instead!)

When he spoke about bonds, he was talking about the exchange of electrons, but at the time I only dimly understood it. He also spoke about quantum levels, and the way extra energy was needed in order to shift to other levels. I saw the pictures he drew on the blackboard, but it didn't really make sense.

When I got to college, although I failed most of my science classes (all those numbers!), there was one section of one chemistry course that

I completely loved and understood: nuclear chemistry. The electrons dancing back and forth, forming different molecules. The concepts were intriguing and fascinating. It actually made the rest of chemistry make sense, and I wished I could go back and take it all over again with my new understanding. Everything in chemistry depends on electrons zigging and zagging and changing partners in their dance, and on the energy needed to cause the shifts.

A decade after graduating from college, I suffered from an ulcer brought on by having a very successful and stressful career in Information Systems. I went to a hypnotherapy demonstration out of curiosity and to support a friend, and walked out cured permanently from that ulcer. I started a journey to discover how the mind and body could be in harmony and reconciled after the split begun by René Descartes, the French philosopher. Certification in Hypnotherapy and Hypnoanesthesia led to certification in Neurolingusitic Programming (NLP), which was a more efficient way of getting the changes in the mind that were needed. I was blown away and excited to learn about Emotional Freedom Technique (EFT, and also called "Tapping"), which seemed to magically reduce migraines to nearly nothing and removed phobias in just one session. I was able to help people quickly and effectively with their suffering, and move them into relief and comfort if not joy.

The real breakthrough for me came in 2014 when I attended my first sound healing lecture. I'd always wanted to learn about it, and I'd waited for years to see John Beaulieu talk about healing using tuning forks. During his lecture and demonstration, I had a very strange parallel audio-video experience. I saw a kind of sidebar overlaying him with pictures and text, and a VOICE telling me, "you're going to record this fork pair as an audio file, and you're going to call it Sweet Sound of Sleep, and you're going to use this trio of forks with EFT in this way to resolve allergic reactions, and this is just the beginning." Now, I've always been a mystic, I've had nudges and "feelings" all my life, and I've been very successful as a Tarot Consultant. But this was way beyond most of my experiences! However, I wasn't going to argue. I recorded the tuning forks and you can find them on my website as the Sweet Sound of Sleep. I do help people resolve their allergies, usually within one appointment, using that trio of tuning forks and EFT. Then one year later, I met Eileen McKusick and learned about Biofield Tuning™. The training in sound healing that she gives goes beyond merely using sound as a healing modality. I was able to remember my college classes and integrate biology, chemistry, and physics into a grand healing package.

Everything is chemistry. You can't escape chemistry, nor chemicals. Even Einstein said, "Chemistry trumps physics." Chemicals make up the entire universe: the air you breathe, the chair you sit on, the floor you stand on, the print you're reading right now (no matter the format), your clothes, your body—everything! And all things vibrate either faster or slower, depending on the molecules or atoms involved. Solids tend to vibrate very slowly, liquids somewhat faster, and gases even faster. Plasma, the fourth state of matter, vibrates the fastest, so fast you rarely see it for more than a second (think of lightning flashes). Electricity can be defined as the presence and flow of electrons in one direction, i.e., a kind of chemistry with boundaries. Even thoughts have vibration, because they are the result of chemical interactions and electricity. The vibrations go out into the universe and either repel or attract other people or things.

It all works because your brain contains a super-busy electro-chemical factory, producing thoughts (electricity, via neurons) and emotions (neurochemicals, from a whole variety of sources). Scientists still debate about which happens first, thoughts or emotions (kind of like the chicken and the egg), but they're both present and active all the time. Of course, your heart also produces electricity (that's how EKGs work), and even your gut churns out its share of electricity and neurochemicals.

Emotions get converted to electricity as part of the chemical process, and electrons quiver and shake and boogie down, causing vibrations everywhere in your body. The result: an electro-magnetic field surrounding you in all directions, extending out three feet or so from the center of your body. This is your biofield.

Most of the vibes coming off you dissipate into your biofield. But powerfully held thoughts and emotions linger and distort the field, creating loops of stuck energy. Your cells pick up the vibrational energy of the thoughts and emotions, and *they* get distorted.

Here's an example. Let's say that you have one or more siblings (or best friends, if you're an only child). Let's say that when you were somewhere between one and five years of age, your sibling or friend broke something that you really loved and treasured. That's a bad enough betrayal, but let's take it farther into the dark side: what if one or the other of your parents took the sibling's part and let them get away with it, or even supported them?

That right there spikes the emotional load and causes a distortion in your biofield. From then on, you're very likely to believe that others will betray you and never support you. Depending on how your brain is wired, you may become a "Pleaser" or an "Antagonist." You may end up with physical symptoms that force others to take care of you or put your needs first. Or you become the "Betrayer," pre-empting any others from betraying you. The distortion affects how you perceive and understand the world, and you end up repeating the situation of betrayal and lack of support over and over again. Every time you do, the distortion gets more and more stuck, as you gather more "evidence."

Here's some of the common distortions you may have encountered:

- Wanting to leave toxic situations, but can't
- Feeling apprehensive about taking the next step(s)
- Challenges with attachments/inability to let go
- Busyness/overdoing/overthinking
- Wanting and never getting
- Frustration/disappointment
- Constant anger/fear
- Guilt/shame
- Feeling powerless
- Continual frustration/disappointment
- Saying yes when you mean no
- Saying no when you mean yes
- Repressing what you want to say
- Continual sadness/depression
- Speaking but not being heard
- Being stuck in the past
- Worrying about the future
- Constant issues with time management

But wait! All is not lost! The distortions in your biofield can be re-tuned and the stuck energy released, so that you can have a life of happiness and prosperity, with fewer roadblocks and emotional challenges.

How does it work? The stuck energy patterns are electrical, generated by the chemistry in your brain, heart, and gut. All it takes is adding coherent energy to make the electrons dance with a different, more useful partner. The trick is *sustaining* the required energy. Many times, I hear a person say, "Oh, I've tried that but it didn't work." It's similar to if you went to the gym only three times for an hour each time, but didn't observe any change in your body. You could say going to the gym didn't work: you would be right because you didn't sustain the energy to have the changes you want.

You may have heard that it takes 21 days to change a habit. It usually takes that much sustained and focused energy to release the electrons from "baditttude" jail so they flow properly. Most of the healing modalities concentrate energy in some way, which may shorten the time needed. You can change any distorted pattern yourself, but if you're going to do it yourself, the three most effective energies to use are: *Time, Application, and Attention.*

Time: You will need to spend five to twenty minutes on a regular schedule with any technique. Change happens over time—you can't get away from it! For most applications, reserve a short amount of time at the beginning, and build up your stamina to handle longer stretches.

Application: You need to do these properly—at least the first or second time through. For example, if you want to raise your heart rate, you can use a treadmill, a bicycle, or an elliptical machine. But if you go to the gym and **sit** on the treadmill for 10 minutes, you just wasted your gym membership (and you might injure yourself!). Using the equipment or technique in the proper way gives maximum results.

Attention: Most distortions show up as thoughts or observations. You have to notice when they show up, and change their energy state as soon as possible. Increase your awareness of emotional or physical discomfort, or of your emotional state in general. As I mentioned earlier, scientists still have some debate about which came first, the thought or the emotion. Your gentle attention to the signals caused by thoughts and/or emotions will help change the distortions' effect on you.

Getting Grounded (Like a battery!)

Have you ever seen a battery? A little knobby thing sticks out at the top and an indentation lurks at the bottom. Those are the positive and negative poles of the battery. Now, if you just wave a battery around in the air, or roll it across the floor, what happens? Nothing, right? You've used energy from your body to move it, but the battery does nothing itself.

But what happens when you add the battery to a radio, or a toy car, or a flashlight? You put the battery in and connect the positive and negative poles with little metal bits, and then the flashlight gets its juice! However, if you don't connect the positive and negative poles to the right connectors, nothing happens, the same as if you've waved it around in the air. Until the battery is properly connected and grounded, the electrons won't flow.

You are a battery! You have positive and negative poles, and most of the time they're completely disconnected. Your negative pole (not a judgment, just the language used to describe electricity) is called the Earth Star. Your positive pole is called the Sun Star. When you connect them together, you increase your sense of being grounded not only to the planet but to all the Universe. Check out my video meditation (and PDF version, if you want to record yourself): **https://bit.ly/BTelectric**

Sue Wilhite

Sue Wilhite specializes in getting her clients unstuck and encouraging them to fulfill their own destinies. She's a best-selling author, Law of Attraction coach, and sound healer. She spent over a decade of her early career in various IT departments doing programming and database design in the Silicon Valley, resulting in a healing crisis in the form of an ulcer. Sue decided it was time to switch gears and go into business for herself. After working for and owning businesses large and small, including running an independent bookstore, Sue found that her biggest passion is helping entrepreneurs get over their money blocks so they can have a thriving business, leading to her nickname as the "Profit Attraction Master." Sue is known as a brilliant and inspiring speaker, and loves to make difficult or complex subjects understandable and relatable.

Sue's digital business card: **https://sue2go.com**
www.facebook.com/SweetSoundofSuccess/
www.twitter.com/positively
www.instagram.com/positivelysuccess/?hl=en
www.linkedin.com/in/suewilhite/
Video demo link mentioned in chapter: **https://bit.ly/BTelectric**

Enjoy your journey to health & a Joyful Life
Rayna

TRUST YOUR INTUITION: YOUR SELF-CARE SUPERPOWER TO HEAL, BALANCE, AND TRANSFORM YOUR LIFE!
BY RAYNA LUMBARD

Self-care covers many facets of our lives: caring for our minds, bodies, emotions, finances, careers, and relationships—our overall health and well-being!

Since the 2020 pandemic hit the planet, we have been dealing with major changes and restrictions that have become our new reality, our shared experiences. "We are all in this together" is the mantra connecting us. We have been shaken to our very core of existence, some more than others. This has manifested for many as heightened anxiety, depression, despair, and stress beyond our normal daily lives. Our self-care practices are more paramount now that *our personal and professional worlds have been challenged in profound ways*. Social justice awareness has mobilized the masses to take more decisive action for transforming us globally to love, not hate. For most of us, these chaotic times are not only scary, but threaten our mental, physical, financial, and emotional well-being. Our souls long for wholeness, the freedom to connect more deeply, to safely touch one another, to love without limits, and to experience inner peace and joy.

There is good news! Many of us are finding our way out of the intense fear, sadness, grief, and anger energy around us, and within us, by safely allowing our feelings to be acknowledged and expressed. Forgiving those we blame for causing this devastation and letting go of the past helps to focus us on what we can control. This is our invitation to be grateful for surviving, have faith, and be nurtured by our safe social bubble. It is time to embrace what we can do now to continue healing through our intuitive knowing.

Who or what supported you emotionally, financially, and/or physically during the 2020 pandemic or another crisis?

What is intuition? It is that part of you we call your inner-wisdom and higher knowing? When you access it through self-awareness, you will trust yourself to make the best decisions for your health and wholeness. When you are open and allowing, you will receive messages from your emotions, body and higher mind. Being in pain is an invitation to alleviate your suffering and receive healing. Your intuition teaches you self-love and helps you reach out for positive support on a higher level than your lower mind that keeps you stuck in fear and past negative experiences. You will hear, know and/or feel awakening "aha messages" that answer vital questions, like why the global reset is happening, and what you are here to learn that will change your life for the best.

If you are feeling like a victim, I invite you to shift your perspective by discovering and learning to trust your intuition known as your Higher Self, Spirit, God, and Source Energy. Being a conduit for higher guidance allows you to know and trust what is best for you. Only you have the answers to be happy and successful. When you really listen to messages from your body tension, disease, imbalance, or painful emotions, your intuition is that still small, or sometimes very loud voice or gut feeling, telling or showing you what's out of balance. Then you can resolve and heal yourself. Acknowledging emotional and physical pain is your wake-up call to "course correct." Seeking out an intuitive therapist will also support you in discovering your subconscious mind's negative programming: what you don't know you don't know! Through inner-awareness, you will discern whether your higher, deeper intuition/wisdom or your painful scary thoughts has your power.

Question: Are you tired of struggling in your relationships, career, finances, having emotional, physical pain, or illness?

Check in with your subconscious negative programs (self-talk) that repeat frequently, like "I'm not good enough," "I'm ugly," "I'm dumb," "I don't deserve success," "I'm not worthwhile," "I'm unlovable," "I'm bad," "I'm not important," or "I don't trust myself." You know what they are! You may need support clearing away negative chatter that rehashes old, obsolete subconscious negative mental programs that trigger painful emotional wounds keeping you stuck!

To heal your childhood (or past lives), invite your own <u>inner</u>-loving parent-self or a positive inner-mother or father you feel safe with to really love and nurture you. This parent is trustworthy and accepts <u>all</u> parts of you unconditionally without being critical or judgmental. With support, your inner-child <u>heals the root causes of your issues</u>, not just your symptoms.

The Causes of My Childhood Trauma—Trusting My Intuition Would be my Loving Guiding Light of Truth

When my world crashed around me as a child, my intuition not only guided me in the best direction, but allowed me to heal my trauma and experience many spiritual awakenings that served me and others and even saved my life!

I was a very energetic, loving, joyful child growing up with my parents and brother. I was also very sensitive to the negative energy in the house, feeling responsible for making everyone happy so that I would feel safe and loved. This was an impossible role to take on. My happy, musical, fun-loving father had been ill with kidney disease "since I was born," my mother would tell me. No one seemed to notice, let alone discuss problems, especially Dad's pain and illness. The denial in the house was palpable. I made the subconscious core decision that it must be my fault he was sick. I must be bad or had done something bad for my father to be in pain. I was determined to make him well so we could be a happy family. I started a healing mission—hearing inner, higher messages that I was here to "save the world." Since my mother and I were not bonded at birth, my father was my world! So as a young child, I did my best to save him—an impossible feat!

I was only nine when he died leaving me heartbroken and feeling very alone. My world fell apart. I was the only one in the family not allowed to go to his funeral, which traumatized me greatly. I fell into a deep depression, and no one really noticed or reached out to me. I was unable to speak up for myself, praying for God to bless my father every day. That comforted me, easing some of my pain and loss by feeling his love. Sometimes I missed my dad so much I prayed that God take me so I could feel his arms around me. Fortunately, God and my angels protected me. I am still sad that we did not share more time together, especially our love for music. During the day, he was busy running our family furniture store with my domineering mother and played music on the weekends.

My mother worked hard to make ends meet and was a fun, positive person to people outside our family. She took good care of our physical necessities and activities, but lacked empathy and compassion toward us. My brother aligned with her against me, having resented me from birth. I felt powerless, but survived being as friendly and caring as possible toward everyone and expressing my acceptance of others to feel okay about myself. Due to my emotional abuse and neglect, I lost some of my grounding and probably would have been on Ritalin if it had been available! I was either really outgoing, headstrong, and confident, or quiet, scared, and depressed. Being the proverbial teacher's pet helped me get noticed, giving me a path to excel and become valedictorian. My intuition became my saving grace. I knew school was my ticket to my self-esteem. I was determined to be perfect, so naturally I poured myself into my studies. Even though I had problems socially, I focused on becoming a dental hygienist and getting away from my mother.

Becoming intuitive was God's gift for dealing with the trauma of losing my father so young. My healing gifts grew stronger through the years. I read people's thoughts and energy easily and received information from Spirit, which helped me excel throughout my life. I really did not know how to explain this phenomenon until I became a marriage and child counselor in my thirties. I now knew how to meditate and express my feelings! I could overcome the pain of being emotionally triggered in my relationships. I no longer felt misunderstood, invisible, and rejected. I had a divine mission ahead of me, a higher plan for my life that included using my intuitive brilliance to serve others and the planet!

Questions: Have you ever experienced emotional or physical trauma, pain, depression and/or anxiety?

Who did you turn to for help? What did you learn from that experience? What wisdom can you share with others dealing with emotional trauma, depression, or anxiety?

I was fortunate enough to have a close relationship with God early on through my Jewish faith. Even though my mother wanted to "get rid of me" on Sunday mornings, *even on our vacations,* I was happy to connect with God at religious school. In 7th grade I read the book *The Still, Small Voice: The Story of Jewish Ethics, by William B. Silverman,* which had a profound effect on me. My intuition even took me to the exact place I needed to write my chapter! I was inspired by "The Voice of the Psalmist, The Holiness of Man," circa 1963, which can be paraphrased to mean "The Holiness of People." "The Voice of God" section can be summarized thusly: "If we listen closely, perhaps we will hear the voice of God speaking to *we who are more fortunate,* asking how are we helping the hungry, the weak, the troubled, the oppressed, the enslaved, and those who yearn for freedom?" I learned the importance of being responsible, devoting myself to helping all people regardless of their race or religion. This spiritual message landed deep into my heart and soul at age 12, as I decided that I was "but a little lower than the angels, created in the image of God." Even though I had been verbally and emotionally abused and neglected by my family, I realized I *must be worthy of being part of God.* I had another "aha" moment, a spiritual awakening born out of emotional pain and loss. Deep down I found it so easy and comforting to listen and trust God and my power of intuition.

Spiritual Awakenings—Embodying Love from God/Spirit

At age 24, I had disabling pain in my fingers from working on dental patients after only two years. I was estranged from my mother and brother and feeling so alone. My "aha" moment came when the doctor told me, "Rayna, there is nothing physically wrong with you!" A flash of lightning shot through me, and I knew instantly I was ready for a dramatic course correction of self-love. My intuition, Spirit, was telling me that it was time to do what I really wanted to do, become a psychotherapist. My life fell into place more easily and effortlessly as I was able to work as a hygienist part-time to support my lifestyle while attending graduate school.

Even though I struggled emotionally and socially into my twenties, I felt God's grace and began trusting that my life had meaning. Even though I had several serious car accidents over the years, I was never injured. During my darkest times, I felt empowered to keep going, not knowing where that would take me. I experienced divine inspiration and intervention through positive thoughts, which enabled feelings of bliss. I knew

I was destined to use my talents and gifts to heal myself and fulfill my divine life purpose. I could choose to struggle or to take the higher road to health and wholeness.

My soul's calling expanded as I became a masterful hypnotherapist, as well as energy and sound healer. I love to share my unique healing gifts as a way to join others, and in doing so, make the world a more loving, compassionate, joyful, happy, and abundant place to thrive.

As a student of life, wife, mother, and now grandmother, I have learned to truly listen and trust my intuition, God's/Spirit's highest guidance. I have total faith that everything works in divine order in the universe and in our lives. Owning my voice and breaking through my musical blocks allowed me to enjoy singing in several community choirs! I am so grateful!

I invite you to love yourself by letting go and healing past destructive childhood programming to unblock your creativity and envision, feel, know, and believe you can and will manifest your happy, healthy, loving, joyful, and abundant future.

Questions: Are you personally and professionally fulfilled in your life right now?

Do you trust your intuition to give you the answers as to why you are fulfilled or not? Are you ready to pursue your dreams?

I invite you to relax in a comfortable place with a pillow or stuffed animal. Take a few deep breaths to connect with your heart. Imagine what your life will look like and how you will feel when you deeply honor your intuition, your innate talents, and gifts. Set your intention to be true to your essence, then call in your healing angels or guides to clear away blocks to your Higher Self. Listen and open all your senses to truly feel and know what is best for your life guided by Spirit! Now you have the power to co-create with Spirit and the right people to support you realizing your dreams!

AFFIRMATIONS: I TRUST that my intuition operates in accordance with the natural laws of the universe. I have total faith that Spirit (God, Source Energy...) is always guiding me to answers that are for my highest good. I am guided to create the best outcome for all involved. For this I am grateful! Thank you! Thank you! Thank you! And so, it is! Ahhh Men and Ahh Women!

Whatever the outcome of this pandemic, your self-care, your **innate spark of divinity,** and deep inner-knowing will teach you the lessons your soul came to the planet to learn. Through God's love for all of us, I know in my heart of hearts **all is well in our universe.**

Rayna Lumbard

Rayna Lumbard, MA, licensed marriage and family therapist, psychospiritual energy/sound healer, and master hypnotherapist creator InnerSuccess Transformations. She inspires and supports you to Transform Your Life for GOOD! Experience her powerful breakthrough technologies, "Inner Wisdom Healing Journey" and "Higher Light Connections."

She is the author of numerous publications including, "Empowering Your Divine Life Purpose," which is the lead chapter in *Authentic Alignment,* and "Dolphins! Adventures in Transformation and Healing," in *Animal Legacies,* an international bestseller on Amazon.

Rayna channels personal messages and sound healing through her Higher Self, angels, archangels, dolphins, and light beings. She loves to heal trauma to allow soul transmissions to guide your divine path to enlightened action. Rayna specializes in individuals and couples online and safely in person on the beautiful Saratoga Creek. She invites you to manifest more love, joy, abundance, and bliss!

Are you ready to . . .

Connect with your Higher Self and spiritual guidance through your Higher Self to open your intuition and telepathic channels?

Raise your vibration by receiving healing light energy and profound messages?

Experience the power of quantum transformation on all levels: health, relationships, career, and finances?

Clear past painful blocks and traumas in your life?

Discover and express your soul's divine purpose and mission to manifest your dreams and serve humanity at this critical time in humanity's evolution?

> *"I so enjoyed Brenda's radio show and loved hearing Rayna share her presence and power from her deep intuition, contributing so much to the listeners! Rayna has an innate connection with Spirit and shares this wisdom in a beautiful, gentle way with an awareness of supporting people's journeys."*
> –Trish Regan, Co-founder of Dolphin\Spirit of Hawaii

Rayna Lumbard, MA, LMFT
InnerSuccess Transformations
Mind/Body/Spirit/Soul Therapy and Healing
20688 Fourth Street, Suite 8
Saratoga, CA 95070
408-605-9195
Rayna@InnerSuccess.com
www.InnerSuccess.com
www.facebook.com/rayna.lumbard InnerSuccess Transformations
www.LinkedIn.com Rayna Lumbard, LMFT

NATURE AS A GUIDING ORACLE
BY TELA TALISE

"Knock, knock, knock!" My bedroom window shook and rattled. I was snuggled up in my mountain of soft blankets. My delicious caramel macchiato coffee went splashing as I leapt to the window three feet from my comfy sanctuary. I slowly peeked out the closed blinds and witnessed a red-bellied woodpecker who was repeatedly banging on the glass. He finally stopped as he heard me open the rest of the blinds and, after a brief face-to-face acknowledgement, flew away. Nature is full of symbols and signs awaiting to be discovered and appreciated. Sometimes those signs are smack in our face, other times we need to look a little more closely. Let's just say that woodpecker came to remind me that I have an opportunity to help others and it was time to share my message now.

In the midst of my bedroom visitor, I was deep in thought about my past. In my mid-thirties, I found myself struggling to find meaning in life. I was in survival mode, lost in all my roles as wife, mother, graduate student, and a full-time worker juggling several jobs. More personal events flooded in, that included relationship heartbreaks, financial struggle, and a diagnosis of depression. Together, they became the final push for me to seek help for the anxiety plaguing me. I did not realize how important self-care was, or even what self-care looked like for me, at this time. I just knew what made me happy: family, nature, animals, and creating things.

So, I cleaned the dust off my acrylic paints that had been buried for over a decade, and decided to try intuitive art. I allowed whatever manifested on the canvas to be my personal art therapy. I created one of my first mandalas, and in the process, I asked for a sign to help me start my journey out of depression. My hand graced the canvas, line after line, until hummingbird appeared and became the symbol of my artwork. For the next few days, hummingbird images came pouring into my life. I saw them on social media, on the television, and even heard someone talking about this tiny, yet symbolic messenger of enjoying the sweetness in life. Curious why this one nature symbol was flooding my life, I came across a book on spirit animal messengers and realized I had found my first animal guide. The symbol of the hummingbird provided animal medicine that opened my world to using self-awareness to access nature as a guiding oracle for self-care. Seeing just how empowering nature can be, I became immersed in finding the deeper meaning of symbols as more animals came into my life and continued to support me in my self-care journey.

The woodpecker provides the message and symbolism of getting back in rhythm and offers an opportunity to do this by literally knocking at your door, or in my case, window! This message was not just for me, but also for you, the reader. "Knock, knock, knock!" This is now your opportunity to learn how nature can guide you in your own self-care journey. Are you ready to meet the rest of your animal symbols and guides? First, let us discover the magic behind how the symbolic aspect of nature works in our self-care journey.

Animal Symbols as Mind and Body Self-Care

"Until you make the unconscious conscious, it will
direct your life and you will call it fate."
—Carl Jung

Working with nature opens the door to our unconsciousness through the universal language of symbols. Each animal and their symbols that repetitively shows up, mirror back something that is needed to awaken our conscious self-awareness. How we view, respond, and feel about animal messengers and their symbols can help us to get to know our authentic selves, which is at the heart of personalized self-care.

The magic of how symbols relate to self-care is that they help us ask those self-discovery questions. Remember when the hummingbird repeatedly came into my life when I was questioning how to get out of my depressive mindset? With hummingbird being a symbol of seeking out the sweetness in life, I questioned what brings me joy and started being more self-aware about doing things that help me maintain a healthier joy-mindset.

Animal Medicine as Soul Self-Care

The soul magic of working with symbols relates to the animal medicine gifted by an animal guide messenger. Animal spirit messengers are also known as animal guides. These symbolic messengers have the gift of animal medicine to offer us as they come in and out of our lives depending on the direction we are headed, goals we have, and the challenges we encounter. For example, woodpecker came in when I needed a reminder to get back into the rhythm of the present moment. I define animal medicine as the healing awareness and energy that a particular animal species brings to our consciousness. This awareness provides a message for guidance, strength, support, inspiration, confirmation, and empowerment.

Finding Your Symbols and Guides through Synchronicities

When we learn to observe repeating patterns or meaningful sightings known as synchronicities, we are gifted with messages that offer animal medicine for our growth and guidance. Our animal guides and symbols can gain our attention in many ways, such as in dreams, meditations, hearing or seeing the animal in-person, or through an overheard conversation, the radio, television, seeing the animal on a bus advertisement, magazine, or during a shamanic journey. Your animal guide can also show up as a symbol of what it is, such as a horseshoe, shark tooth, or feather, just to name a few. Any combination of these sightings in a short period of time is your "ah ha" moment to start the message decoding process.

When you see the same animal guide or symbol of that animal on repeat occasions, pay attention and write it down. I recommend keeping a journal to track your observations. One of my meaningful synchronicities started with a dream of a brown horse. The following day I was driving and saw a rider on a brown horse at the red light. Then, the next day I turned on the television to a movie about horses. This was two days and three symbols. Other times it took me a few weeks to get the message! Usually when you get the message, your animal guide will go on its way. However, don't be surprised if they visit you again because you need reminding of the teaching or medicine they offer. Horse is one that frequently jumps into my life when I need confidence in facing workload challenges. In this situation, I was trying to decide on whether to leave a challenging job and how I would find another that offered more freedom. Horse symbolizes adventure, breaking free, and jumping over obstacles. This message gave me confirmation in my self-care that breaking free from this job was best for me. It was! Within the month, I no longer needed that position and landed another opportunity that offered what I needed. When horse symbols started showing up during my job search, I questioned my ability to push past the unease of leaving a draining but good paying job. I asked questions regarding what was holding me back. This animal guide challenged me to take that leap into a new adventure.

How to Decode your Messages

Decoding the messages is all about building a relationship with your animal messengers. How do you do this? Like any relationship, you get to know them. First, you need to reflect on the characteristics of the animal and decide what it symbolizes personally to you. Then, research the animal and find its characteristics and unique traits. Looking at books or online animal symbolism after you do your own reflections will give you more clues to your personal message. Finally, take inventory of what is going on in your life and how you feel toward this animal symbol. Your personal feelings, emotions, and perspective of the sign is part of decoding the message. Once you have the symbolism through your own perspective and the research you did, you can get to the juicy part. Are you ready? It is asking those questions about your own self-care. Here is an exercise to help you do just that!

Journal Activity: Animal in the Mirror

1. Think of an animal or the symbols of the animal that you've frequently observed lately and make your animal's name the title of your entry.

2. Write down 2-3 reflections of what this animal symbolizes to you without looking up the meaning. Also include how you feel about the animal. *For example: Raccoon wears a mask. Raccoons look like they are in disguise and are curious.*

3. Now write 2-3 more symbols this animal represents by looking up the animal by either searching online for the meaning of your animal messenger guide or looking at a book on animal symbolism. *For Example: Raccoon Symbolism - Playfulness, Secrecy and Adaptable.*

3. Write down your current situation. Are you going through any challenges? Do you have any projects or goals? *For example: At your new job you are hesitant of making friends because the last job someone took credit for the big project you did on your own.*

4. Time to look in the mirror! What questions can you ask yourself to understand the animal messenger based on what it represents and the feelings you have toward it? *For Example: Are my fears of another person taking my work again hindering my success at the new job? What can I do to remove my own mask and secrecy and be more authentic and sociable in my job?*

In this exercise you took personal inventory of what you needed to focus on based on the animal symbol that showed up for you. By asking questions, you make the unconscious, conscious! By writing your reflections down, you acknowledge what you can do to improve your self-care in each situation, and in the process, improve your self-awareness.

Inviting Animal Messengers into Your Life

Signs and messages do come without our request. The repeat observations are part of the animal guides' mission to help make the unconscious, conscious. They bring opportunities for growth, healing, and evolution to your path by showing up for you. You can also invite animal guides into your life based on what you're working on in your self-care journey.

When you get to know what the animal guides and symbols mean to you and see what lessons and "specialties" they bring into your life, you can ask certain animal guides to work with you. Here are some of the animal guides that I have fostered relationships with for their symbolic focus areas.

Bison – Abundance, Gratitude, Grounding

Owl – Intuition, Wisdom, Study, Observation

Otter – Joy, Creativity, Playfulness

Seahorse – Contentment, Persistence, Generosity, Patience

Whale – Connecting to the Heart, Healing, Communications

Woodpecker – Opportunity, Getting Back to Your Rhythm, Awareness

I want to note that each animal guide I listed is not limited to the symbolism shared. The more you get to know your animal guides or spirit animals, the more symbolism you will discover. The next activity I created to help you invite animal guides into your life based on a personal need.

Self-Care Animal Guide Invocation

Set your intention. This can be done by saying a personal request or using the example mantra below:

I welcome and invite (name of animal guide) wisdom into my life for self-care and inspiration to (write your challenge or goal). Thank you for your guidance and inspiration.

Example: I welcome and invite <u>otter's</u> wisdom into my life for self-care and inspiration to <u>help me find more creativity in my new book project</u>. Thank you for your guidance and inspiration.

By inviting guides in, you are also taking the time to honor nature and yourself as you are both connected. The purpose of this exercise is to help you focus your energy and help you be more observant of nature's symbols.

Mandala by Tela Talise

Intention Setting Exercise:
Focus on the mandala and say your intention.
"I welcome and invite Woodpecker wisdom into my life for the opportunity to open up my awareness to my guides, symbols and messages. Thank you for your guidance and inspiration."

Honoring your Messages

Once you discover and decode your own personal messages from nature, I have the practice of giving gratitude. Not only does giving gratitude foster the relationships with your animal guides, it also honors you in the process. You are the one looking in the mirror, right? Working with nature as a guiding oracle for self-care has several lasting impacts such as:

Working with nature symbols helps you in doing your shadow work. This means you are looking at nature as a mirror to help you reflect on things that need to be brought to the conscious mind for personal healing through the symbols that prompt those personal questions. This process builds a better relationship with yourself.

Gratitude is awareness. Conscious awareness is self-care. There is no one way to express gratitude.

Here are ways to honor you, your symbols and animal messengers:

1. **Say "thank you" in any way that makes you happy.** This could be feeding the birds, volunteering at an animal sanctuary, or supporting an animal rescue fundraiser.

2. **Create an art or a vision board of the animal messenger.** Write, journal, create a song, or any other creative endeavor that allows you to have the intention of thankfulness.

3. **Keep a symbol of the animal with you.** This could be wearing a shirt with the image of your animal symbol, or having a necklace, carving, or picture of your animal. This is one of my favorite ways to honor animal messengers and why I have an online store dedicated to this!

4. **Watch or read about your animal messengers.** Remember, the more you know about your animal and animal symbols, the better the relationship.

You may find you already do some of these practices unconsciously. Our ancestors have been doing this process of honoring nature from the beginning of recorded history. Animals have inspired, supported, and guided humans for thousands of years. It is a relationship that works.

"Hummingbird was the first spirit animal to come through in my intuitive paintings. This guide became the start of my awareness of the healing power of symbols." – Tela Talise

My Invitation to You!

Nature is your oracle and this chapter is a taste of how fun it can be to be awakened to animal messengers and their symbols as part of your self-care journey! I love hearing about my readers' nature-inspired stories! I invite you to share with me what animal messages flow into your life and what unconscious things you made conscious on your path to nature inspired self-care. As a gift to help you create a dedicated self-care practice, visit **http://www.mypathinspired.com/about** for a free meditation coloring sheet and more nature inspired resources to empower you on your self-care journey.

Tela Talise is a professional artist, entrepreneur, educator, and self-care coach. She is also a college professor holding multiple degrees and certifications in fine arts, illustration, leadership, management, and education. She is a trained reiki master, experienced in trancework, meditation, symbolism, and the intuitive arts. In 2015, she founded her passion and business, My Path Inspired, to provide vibrant, symbolic nature-based art to the world and to inspire people to learn how symbolism and self-awareness are part of self-care and personal empowerment. She is an advocate for depression-awareness and shows the world the power of nature inspired self-care as a way for living with more joy and abundance. She has the unique gift for teaching others how to work with symbols and spirit animals on a spiritual and psychological level.

Tela is known for her layers of symbolism in her paintings and often jokes about the line of spirit animals awaiting their portraits. She is in the progress of creating a personal empowerment inspirational card deck that her patrons eagerly await! She loves facilitating workshops on learning about spirit animals and totems. When she is not creating or teaching, she can be found among the sunflowers in the garden, bird watching, hiking, or admiring the waves at the beach. She resides in New Jersey with her husband, daughter, and son.

One of her favorite quotes is...

"The better you know yourself, the better your
relationship with the rest of the world."
—*Toni Collette.*

Do you have an animal or nature inspired story that empowered your self-care journey? She loves to hear from her patrons and readers. She invites you to share your own inspirational symbols and how her chapter supported you in the gift of self-care through self-awareness.

Business email: **mypathinspired@gmail.com**
Website: **http://www.mypathinspired.com**
Etsy store: **http://www.etsy.com/shop/mypathinspired**
Facebook: **http://www.facebook.com/mypathinspired**
Instagram: **http://www.instagram.com/mypath9**

ALLOWING YOUR TRUE SELF TO FLOURISH
BY MEGAN MURPHY

It took a momentous event to start uncovering my true self. While bringing new life into this world is commonplace, giving birth to my first child threw my purpose and sense of self into question and unleashed a mid-life crisis. I felt angry that other parents had not been more honest with me about the challenges that raising a child could bring. I felt unable to simultaneously hold this new role and my previous roles, too—there wasn't enough time in the day to do it all. I began seeking support from an energy healer, a type of support that was entirely new to me, and began my journey in redefining myself. This involved developing a meditation practice, seeking out books on spirituality, and discovering that my purpose in this life does not fit within the space of a job title. I think it is human nature to desire a title or clear role that gives us meaning and it is an uncomfortable space to be in when you don't know what your title is. However, a job title does not allow for being an expansive and creative individual who is always unfolding. It is through developing a meditation practice that I have tapped the intuitive, emerging person that I am, enabling me to quiet my self-sabotaging ego that diminishes my gifts. Thus, I have retrained my mind to think thoughts that uplift and empower me to embrace my true self.

After taking the plunge into motherhood, my husband and I moved from Alaska to my family's centennial farm in Illinois. I now grow medicinal plants, craft flower essences, and develop wellness products. I never would have anticipated coming back to the area where I grew up, nor would I have envisioned being a creator of plant-based medicine. And now it makes complete sense to me as I continue to follow my heart. The process of living into your true self is one you get to define and the roadmap on how to do this is within you. We each have the opportunity to reclaim our power and step into our best selves. When we know that we have this power within us, it is a matter of finding the tools that best resonate with our spirit—tools that enable us to quiet our mind, go within ourselves, and celebrate our worth. So, the following paragraphs offer just a few ways to do this, and fortunately, are amongst many others in this book so you can see what works best for you.

This chapter offers two ways to allow your true self to flourish: 1. A process that helps you observe your emotions so that you can intentionally respond to your life experiences instead of aimlessly react to them, and 2. A process that uses the *Ammi visigna* (Ammi) flower essence and self-reflection questions to catalyze ascension and self-realization. With the ability to choose your responses, you can raise your consciousness and attract more positive thoughts, behaviors, and experiences into your life. Using flower essences can also support you in raising your consciousness while also assisting the body and mind in letting go of experiences that do not serve you. The Ammi flower essence can specifically help you uncover and empower your true self.

If you are reading this book, you can celebrate your ability to attract support tools into your life! Thankfully, the most important tools for this life's journey are those with which every individual is born: our emotions. Our emotional guidance system is our most powerful, inherent tool for actualizing our true self. Most cultures and societies do not fully utilize the power of this emotional guidance system and, unfortunately, diminish it. Awareness of our emotions unlocks the self-empowered ability to choose our thoughts and how we respond to them. We can ultimately choose how we feel by acknowledging the thoughts and feelings that we have and then determining if these thoughts or feelings are serving us. The practice of choosing the thoughts to which we give energy and attention is an exercise of observation. This practice does not encourage one to ignore experiences or emotions that are uncomfortable, but rather to have compassion for the thoughts and feelings that one experiences and then to choose a response that feels best. When we create space in our life to observe our thoughts and emotions, we will find that there are ample opportunities to retrain our brain and have more positive experiences. A great deal of time is typically spent analyzing and worrying about things that ultimately do not impact one's well-being, however, the energy spent on them does. Energy can be redirected to ideas and inspired action when you allow yourself to let go of worry and self-doubt. It involves training one's self-compassion muscle so that one's humanness is acknowledged and one tries again until a better response is experienced.

Every individual's emotions are their first signs of whether or not they are in alignment with their spirit. Alignment is a unique position where one's body, mind, and spirit are on the same page with one another and the individual is experiencing life with a unified team. Being in alignment is inherently natural when you allow your feelings to guide your choices. This enables one to focus on and recognize the experiences that will bring joy and foster one's sense of worthiness. Paying attention to our emotional guidance system, or emotions, is our most important gauge for whether or not we are aligned with our highest ideals for our self. When we are aware of our feelings, we can more readily fine-tune our response so that we are in a place of alignment more often than not. This practice of fine-tuning your thoughts to uplift instead of undermine yourself is the foundation for everything you create in your life. Maintaining your self-esteem and valuing your worth is not easy and is the *real* work of becoming your best self. It does require action, but much less is needed when you get out in front of it by prioritizing your self-care. The action is then done with inspiration and there is no better feeling than inspired action.

The secret to successfully uncovering the life you most want to live is to *allow* it to happen.

The art of allowing can be challenging to adopt as we have trained ourselves to create our lives by hard-earned doing, action, and work. We are comfortable with putting in effort in order to obtain tangible results. Allowing, on the other hand, is a different practice of reaching for thoughts that uplift us or soothe us. Much like the practice described by neuro-linguistic programming, when you can detach from the thoughts you are thinking as separate from you, you can then intentionally choose to let go of any self-doubt or criticism that can cloud your most inspired thinking. This does not mean one ignores cues for improvement, rather it is an opportunity to retrain the self-sabotaging ego that tends to emphasize the reasons why one should not follow their heart and take risks of being their true self. When you choose the thoughts that honor your inherent worth, your individuality, your preferences, and your desires, you enable yourself to nourish your inspirations. This art of allowing is not a passive activity, but a very deliberate practice of letting go of drama, thoughts or things that do not feel good, and instead humbly experiencing your most inspired self. With this practice, the focus of your life can be adjusted from any starting point to a place of renewed vitality. Intentionally choosing your thoughts is the foundation for being well and wellness is the foundation for living your most desired life.

Wellness is a balance between harmony and disharmony for which we are always striving. Flower essences facilitate the balancing process within our body, minds, and spirits by helping us identify and remove emotional obstacles that can get in the way of us following our hearts. While it is not necessary to use flower essences to bring about this clearing, they act as a catalyst in reminding our bodies how we feel when we are aligned with our true self. They remind us what it feels like when we do not resist our intuitive guidance, our inner self, and instead allow our heart to guide us. All flower essences are powerful vibrations of specific flowers that are used to remind the human body how it feels to vibrate at a higher frequency. Flower essences are typically created by placing a pristine flower, or its petals, in a glass bowl of water in the sun for a few hours. This process enables the frequency of the flower to be transmitted to the water, as water has the ability to resonate at whatever frequency to which it is exposed (see Masara Emoto's *The True Power of Water*).. After this process is complete, the flower is removed and the water is combined and preserved with alcohol. When an individual takes a drop of this concentrated flower essence, it helps to remind their body how it feels when unobstructed by negative emotions and can enliven their ability to let go of thoughts and feelings that bring them down. Similar to the power of music and its ability to uplift us, every flower has a unique vibration or song that can move us just by being in its presence.

The *Ammi visnaga* flower essence aims to help an individual in reaching for their higher self, their true purpose, and their intuitive gifts. This is the intention of their song: to uplift you into a place where you are inspired to tap your intuitive gifts. Flower essences work in a gentle, subtle manner and allow the human mind to arrive at its own conclusions. It is with a quiet mind that a flower's essence is most effective in reinforcing balance.

While flower essences work without any deliberate action on the part of the receiver, using essences with intention and focusing in on the gifts they offer facilitates increased self-awareness, self-empowerment, and self-realization. Additionally, utilizing self-reflection questions alongside the essences can help dislodge and bring attention to memories, emotions, or beliefs that can obstruct your higher vibrations. These questions can also serve any individual regardless of their use of the essences, however, the essences provide lubrication to one's ability to conjure up and release limiting emotions and beliefs. The goal of each question is to provoke the individual to use their emotional guidance system, acknowledge any obstructions that come up, release these obstructions, and then allow oneself to fully experience the feelings of:

Actualization – the ability to manifest your visions

Applause – the ability to celebrate an individual's or another's accomplishments

Solitude – the ability to lean in to your own power to guide you

Selflessness – the ability to let go of any desire for acknowledgment and/or reciprocation

Integrity – the ability to acknowledge your own true nature, needs, and desires while also respecting the same needs of others

Alignment – the ability to connect with your highest self and follow your true path

Serenity – the ability to experience peace in all that surrounds us

Joy – the ability to experience pleasure from noticing the beauty that surround us

Gratitude – the ability to experience appreciation in and for all that sustains and supports us

Honesty – the ability to experience truthfulness with your own spirit and journey

Sincerity – the ability to communicate truthfulness with yourself and to others

Peace – the ability to experience complete satisfaction with all that is and will ever be

These 12 ways of feeling are a phenomenal bar for gauging our best-feeling self and provide a North Star for us to follow. When we genuinely experience these feelings, we know we are in alignment and on the path of our most desired life.

The capacity to heal oneself and live in to one's full potential is a power that needs to be reclaimed. This day and age provides abundant access to self-empowerment tools and support, however, the decision is up to the individual to take the reins and find the tools that best enable them to flourish. If you would like to learn more about the process described above, access more information about the Ammi flower essence, or download free self-reflection questions, please visit **backyardbeauty.net**.

Many blessings to you on your journey—may you find the tools to support your ongoing expansion and align with your true self.

Best,

Megan Murphy and her team of guides

Megan Murphy

Megan Murphy is a practiced scientist and naturalist who has recently discovered her own intuitive healing abilities. She uses these gifts to create flower essences, craft body and skin care products, and develop self-care practices for her own and others' well-being. She offers these services, information, and wellness products through her business, Backyard Beauty.

Backyard Beauty's vision is to, "cultivate joy through flowers, art, and self-care," thus Megan aims to support herself and others in seeing and celebrating the beauty in our own backyards, particularly the one of our true self. As a budding herbalist, she also appreciates utilizing the diverse benefits of our backyard plants to support balance in our bodies, minds, and spirits.

Megan has a master's degree in biological oceanography and spent years in Alaska as an environmental educator, researcher, and science communicator. She then coordinated a community wellness coalition in Homer, Alaska for three years. This gave her the opportunity to practice collective impact as a unifying process for addressing socially-complex issues. She now believes this is an integral process for rebuilding our relationships across all scales. After giving birth to her second child, she moved to her centennial family farm in Illinois with her husband and kids to authentically define and practice what wellness means to her.

Email: **backyardbeautyil@gmail.com**
Website: **backyardbeauty.net**
Facebook page(s): @backyardbeautyIL
Instagram: @backyard_beauty_

BECOME BEST FRIENDS WITH YOUR SHADOW
BY SHAUNA CUCH

"You can never realize your true Being unless all the unconscious parts of your illusory identity come to the surface and you recognize them not to be you."
—Santata Gamana

If you had a magic wand, what in your life would you change? That my friend, can be your reality. Life seems to put us on a path that we have no control or say in. Is that true? It is true if you believe it is true. Wouldn't you rather believe in a magic wand? I believe the magic lies within you and your belief system. Imagine if you could take a magic wand and drastically change or disappear that gigantic obstacle in your life FOREVER.

This is truly one of the most important secrets of self-care, getting to know what is really going on within your energy field. You can be the cause of your life rather than have life come at you and be at its mercy. Does this sound daunting? It really is quite a simple shift. You are simply bringing love, light, and awareness to the unknown. Awareness opens the heart. Many of us harshly judge the unknown because we think we are supposed to always be the light and avoid our shadow. On top of that, fear of the unknown keeps us from wanting to explore that mystery within us.

We instinctively want to avoid our fears. So, I am inviting you readers to dive into the unknown with me for the sake of self-care.

Dr. Jeffery L. Finnan, PhD explains it best in his book, *Commanding the Power of Thought*, where he argues that 95% of everything we think, say, and do, comes from the subconscious part of our brain. Only 5% comes from the cortex, or thinking part of our brain. That other 90% that is unknown, I call our shadow side. My challenge to you my friend is to have some fun with me and be willing to discover a part of you that you haven't acknowledged that may be causing you grief or irritation. **I am suggesting that you open your heart and your awareness and become best friends with your shadow!**

Why do we want to become best friends with our shadow? Most of us have heard "what you resist will persist," yet we are not even conscious that we are resisting! The first way to get to know your shadow is to know that you do not know it! That is right, who goes around talking about their shadow? That is not a popular subject, in fact most of us tend to sweep it under the rug, or blame it on someone else, or deny and distract from feeling any of it. That is what keeps us from self-care; our mind tells us we are too busy to go within, meanwhile, we are unconsciously creating the thinking that we are too busy to avoid facing what we do not know about ourselves.

To embrace your shadow is to understand the message behind it rather than to resist or avoid it. There is always something quite beautiful within that deep dark place that can help you learn and grow. Allow me to share with you a little bit about my life.

I grew up in a polygamous family. My dad had three wives and thirty-three children. Dad believed that children were to be seen and not heard. My mother had thirteen children, ten girls and three boys. I was Mom's tenth child and Dad's twenty-ninth child.

My mother always shared with us that she never wanted more than four children, but had them for the sake of religion. Her own abuse as a child caused her to completely shut down her emotions. I inherited her suppressed rage in the womb and her internal storyline of "I can't stop the abuse." She would turn her little toddlers over to my dad for a beating to check their emotions. **I believe I came into their life to confront this behavior.**

At an early age of nine months old, my mom became pregnant with her eleventh child, so she decided to wean me. I would not have it. I would not stop crying from her sudden and abrupt refusal to nurse, I displayed too much emotion for her. She turned me over to my dad at an incredibly young age for the routine spanking. No matter how much my dad beat me for crying, I would not let up. I would cry harder every time I saw him. Unfortunately, my dad had to win, after all, he was the patriarch. **The beatings and confinement to the crib for crying was my life as a child.**

What followed was life as I knew it. As one who was abused, a life of abuse seemed normal. I had no idea that there was such a thing as mental and emotional abuse. I also inherited my mother's suppressed rage that was exacerbated by the beatings. Therefore, I attracted a man with rage issues. I submitted to that rage for twenty-seven years, not realizing that I deserved better. My belief was that I had to work hard for love and money. I was widowed at 42-years-old and I continued to attract men with mother issues that I felt I needed to fix so they could love me. But they were just my mirror. I unconsciously believed there was something wrong with me for having emotions, so I needed fixing. **I was a work-a-holic and a serve-a-holic, keeping myself too busy and distracted to go within and discover what was buried there, discover why I was creating all this difficulty and pain. I managed to live a full life, raise eleven amazing children who are very accomplished, and make huge contributions. Yet, I did not realize the impact of creating from my shadow wounds. I had health issues from all my suppressed emotions that I did not express or even acknowledge.**

Growing up, I had completely shut out any memory, along with the fear and trauma from all the emotional and physical abuse. I knew I had no memory of my childhood, but I did not realize how important it was to uncover this hidden trauma for the sake of my well-being. I stayed busy so I didn't have to deal with my shadow, and I felt justified by my busyness. Another trait that comes from hidden shadow is procrastination. I never realized I was a procrastinator because I was not willing to face the things that needed to be dealt with. **I was unconsciously neglecting my abused and neglected inner-child that believed she was unlovable.**

Just before I learned about my abuse, I had a dream. I rarely remember dreams, but this one was so vivid it became a pivotal point in my life. In the dream, I was driving somewhere in my car and I heard a baby whimper. I glanced in the back seat and there was a little child hidden under stuff! I felt horrible about the neglect; I love babies and I could not believe that someone would do such a thing. I inquired and even demanded consequences for everyone who would neglect a child like this. I had to find out who had left this poor child in the back seat with no love and care. Then I woke up deeply startled and shaken.

There were so many precious learnings from that dream that came into my awareness. Soon after, **I discovered an amazing process designed to clear deep wounds called family constellations.** This is a highly effective method that I describe in detail in my book *Big Souls Make Big Promises.* Through this powerful process, I uncovered an altered and hidden personality that was created from disassociating from my body while I was being abused. This angry child within me had a voice that felt unlovable and was demanding to be heard by speaking out of turn or blurting out hurtful judgments. I had a shadow side of me that I never realized I had, much less took responsibility for. This child was my Christ consciousness, and I had shut it out and neglected to love and care for that inner-child.

I had no memory of this abuse until I turned sixty and got a call from my sisters who I generally avoided because I did not feel seen or heard by them. Our parents had passed, and they wanted us to all meet once a month for lunch. At one of these lunches, they began discussing their one spanking from my dad. I quipped, "I had a great relationship with Dad, I never had any spankings." They looked up at me and said altogether, "Oh yes you did!" That my friend, began my journey into my shadow side that I was completely unaware of; the shadow running my life.

I had come into the family to disrupt this pattern. I challenged my dad daily and paid the price for it but that did not stop me according to my siblings. I had black and blue hand marks all over my body. Not only that, but my mom's rule was also if a baby cries when they have been fed or changed, they belong in the crib or they will be spoiled. So, the crib was my prison for expressing myself. I was rebellious and obstinate and difficult to get along with.

Now granted it may seem like mine is a rare and extreme case, but trauma is trauma no matter how great or insignificant it is. A child's version of life before they turn eight is a very distorted view of reality and one incident can cause a child to create a story of not being loved, or not being enough. My point in sharing this is you do not know what you do not know until you know it! What is lurking in your energy field that keeps you from self-care or being present and still within? How often do you make a promise to yourself that you are going to spend time doing your morning or evening rituals and manage to be too busy to take that time?

We all carry ancestral wounds that are passed down to us, yet we never have shadow greater than our light. **I saw this not only from my own experiences, but as a trained and certified facilitator of family constellations.** Despite this hidden trauma, life was never more than I could bear. I have a gift of faith, so I am an amazing and fearless creator when I set my mind to something. But the effect of this unconscious energy is a low vibration of shame which was creating the self-sabotage from this angry child that had never been seen or heard. Every time I was about to benefit from what I was creating, I lost it in one fell swoop. I created an amazing business, had a million-dollar home, valuable land, and lost it all overnight. This is what finally got me to look within.

I realize my story is not your story, but do you know what emotions or stories are running your life that are begging to be heard? I found in my work as a facilitator that many people carry emotions that do not belong to them. In my opinion, this is one of the most foundational principle of self-care. To know thy self is to know God. My shadow is the part of me I was running from for most of my life. Yet loving that part of me has helped me love my self and find the Creator in me.

Why was I running from my shadow? My upbringing for one. We constantly teach our children to BE GOOD. I was raised to believe you go to hell if your bad and in the darkness, the unknown. It was all considered a part of that scary thought or judgment. Does this mean we should spend our time thinking about the darkness in us all day long? I am suggesting that unconsciously we avoid, distract, deny, or resist our shadow.

We ARE focused on our shadow all day long because we are working so hard not to be that darkness, so we resist it by trying not to be all these characteristics of shadow. Many of us spend our life seeking the light, we have become an array of gifted energy workers getting rid of dark energy. Either that, or we may be avoiding our dark (or shadow) side as if it does not exist, like I did. The shame of our dark side would be more acceptable if other people were bringing their shadow to light without judgment.

In my training in quantum emotional clearing and from working with clients and their resistance to shadow, I eventually saw the need to create a recording of a shadow clearing done with tapping three fingers on the third eye while repeating it out loud . This clearing is highly effective in releasing the shame and other unconscious behaviors that accompany our shadow. I wanted to share it with you in case you want to release shame and learn what might be driving you. You can find this clearing process on my website on the conscious community page under the testimonials: **www.journeyintotheheart.net**

I will share with you one of the most important rituals I teach in my popular **Relationship Alchemy course.** We start out by helping you discover for yourself who you are, and then we keep a journal of who you are not. I call it your shadow journal. **I have found that until you become familiar with who you are not, then you will not have the clarity to turn your back on it and focus on who you are.** This can be done with no resistance and no shame; remarkably simple awareness opens the heart and helps you quit judging yourself and others by projecting your stuff out there. **By owning this part of you, you become empowered enough to embrace it.** This process will inspire you to take charge of your life by encouraging you every time you find yourself in a negative state or triggered by something to look within, feel it, track it, own it, and speak to it.

In my **Relationship Alchemy course,** before we dive into our shadow, we first establish and define who you are: for example, one process is helping you choose your 12 metaphysical I AM qualities. This is who you are creating you to be. This is what you repeatedly use in a mantra as you visualize and meditate. For instance, I say, I AM *love*, and I visualize a light being of love; I AM *freedom*, and I visualize an eagle flying above all the morass; I AM *grace*, and I visualize a queen; I AM *wisdom*, and I visualize a wise medicine woman. I do this every time I need to step into my power and speak my truth boldly, when I feel challenged by a lack of confidence, or when shame around self-expression comes up.

Positive visualization is key, but just as important is awareness of what is. Turn your journal around and upside down and start a journal for your shadow in the back of your journal. This is not typical advice or routine for your self-care, so I have created a special gift for you to make this process simple and easy. I will go into detail on how to create your shadow journal to bring light and awareness to the unknown 95% that may be running your life. I will show you how to discover these hidden gems once you learn how to keep a shadow journal.

Let us start with a deeper understanding of what your shadow is, then we will talk about how it shows up in your life.

Your shadow's job is to stop you from your light, love, and truth.

Your shadow wants you to focus on what or who you are not.

Your shadow convinces you to mask your true authentic self.

Here are some examples of the secrets that hide within your shadow: childhood trauma, ancestral baggage, parental imprint, family patterns, soul wounds, and limiting beliefs.

Shadow can be either subconscious or unconscious. Most importantly, know thy self! Learn how to tap into and ask your higher self (masculine and feminine divine power) to help you identify what is not you, and by contrast, what is truly you. This is our true power; we simply get to learn how to access this part of us. The part of us that is more than ready and willing to do anything we ask. **We default to unconscious behavior while overriding our super power.**

If you have read my book called *Big Souls Make Big Promises*, you know I explain the power of the circle and how it reveals your truth. Many of us are not even accessing the power that lies within, the power that is waiting for us to acknowledge and make use of it. **We are our own most powerful being.** No one is more powerful to you than you are. **We are the only ones that can access and create from that power that lies within us.**

After years of experience in my practice of facilitating family constellations and witnessing shadow work, I have created an effective tool to expose your shadow to the light. I am excited to share this shadow journal to help all of you integrate and find a deeper love. **This is my gift to you. Go to my website and sign up for the free journal. This includes a 30-minute strategy session with me on how to incorporate this process in your self-care routine with ease and grace.**

I hope you find the courage to embrace your shadow and step into your true power and light! I cannot wait to hear about your journey into your heart where you will discover your authentic power and your true identity.

Shauna Cuch

Shauna is founder of Journey into the Heart. She is the author of a number one international best seller called *Big Souls Make Big Promises*. Shauna has a phenomenally successful course called, "Relationship Alchemy" where she helps you find peace of mind amidst the chaos and discover sovereignty of the soul in any given situation. She is also known to assist in uncoupling people in relationships that are toxic in a way that relieves pain without unnecessary drama and expense.

She is trained and certified in systemic healing, also known as family constellations, a method widely used in a multitude of countries that value the work. Her use of a wide variety of specific and dynamic modalities, when coupled with her wisdom, raise the vibration, frequency, and consciousness in the circle. Her approach is unique, individualized, and draws on her years of experience not only in constellations, but in shadow clearing, which is the practice of transmuting darkness to light within our divine energy fields.

Book: Big Souls Make Big Promises is sold on Amazon
Website: **www.journeyintotheheart.net**
Email: **shauna@journeyintotheheart.net**
Facebook: Journey into the Heart
Instagram: Journeyintotheheart7

MY SOUL GOT ME FIRED...
THAT'S CODE FOR FREEDOM!
BY AMANDA SLADE

My Soul got me fired. It was the first day in my New York office. The publishing firm where I worked had shut down our Tampa office and wanted me to move to New York.

Ten years earlier, I would have jumped at the chance to live there. But now I was 40 years old, had built a beautiful custom home in Tampa, Florida, and the last thing I wanted was to live in a shoebox in busy Manhattan.

At the time, I lived by my "shoulds." I really had no clue what I wanted, what I was passionate about, or even why I did the things I did.

I climbed the corporate ladder, and achieved success while making six figures. I was a VP of Sales and Marketing, with a staff of 14, worked 70-80 hours a week, traveled around the country, but I had no personal life. I wasn't happy. All I knew were my "shoulds." I "should" do this or that to succeed in my life.

When the powers that be made the unilateral decision to close the Tampa office, I had to relocate to keep my job and I begrudgingly went to

New York. On January 2, 1997, I woke up startled, after having a strange dream. I shook it off and went into the office at 7 am.

I got my new office set up and visited different departments to check on projects. Slowly but surely, I became more and more upset as I found out my General Manager had undermined everything I had implemented, and didn't consult me before making changes.

At 11 am, we had our weekly phone call together. As we began the call, it was like something came over me. I felt a surge of energy flowing through me from the top of my head, all the way down my body. This energy took over what I was saying.

It wasn't me talking . . . it was my Soul talking. I expressed my frustration about what he was doing. I questioned why he was relocating me to NY and not utilizing my expertise. I called him out for his actions. It was the same thing they had done with my predecessor ... the person had all of the responsibility, but had none of the authority. When I was first offered the position, we had an agreement that I would not be their puppet. I reminded him this is not what I had signed up to do.

It was like a cartoon. As the words tumbled out, I tried to gather them and literally stuff them back in my mouth. Interestingly, I had been stuffing my feelings for eons, so this was nothing new.

It felt like there was another Amanda in the room. This energy and power that was surging through me was amazing. Knowing what I know now, it was my Soul taking over and saying, "Enough is enough. You're done here and it's time to move on."

When I hung up the phone, I thought, "Well, as a marketer this was not the way to keep my job. I just nailed my coffin shut." Two hours later, I was called into the CFO's office and fired.

As I walked out of his office, I immediately felt relief. I thought, "My Soul just got me fired . . . it has set me free!"

I immediately remembered the dream I had earlier in the morning. Its message was that everything would be okay . . . it may be rough for a while, AND I would emerge with the sun shining brightly upon me. I had no idea what that meant, but for some reason, I trusted it.

I had no plan B, and really didn't know what I wanted for my Self. I was well-respected in the industry, so I had many potential opportunities. However, when I went to interview, I sat in my car in the parking lot, crying and feeling totally drained. There was no spark, nor enthusiasm to continue on this career path. I knew something had to change, and a new job was not the answer.

I tumbled into a deep depression. Two months later, I literally fell to my knees in utter despair and asked God for help. And truth be told, I really didn't ask. I *told* God that if things didn't change in six months, I'm out of here (yes, suicide). I let God know I was willing to do anything that would help me and my life to change, just show me the way.

Well, what I *didn't* know is that I had actually asked to be put on a fast track of healing, transformation, and evolution. I'd been on a spiritual path for years, and recently started learning about energetic healing.

I attended workshops, not really understanding what energy was, what a chakra was, but I knew in my heart that I was in the right place. I had no idea what I was doing, but *did* know I always felt better after an energetic healing session.

My exploration was the catalyst for my Soul to take over and show me the way. I felt dead inside for years. When I started with energetic healing, I became alive again. I could feel energy move within me. My feelings started surfacing, so I could recognize when something was off for me.

I resisted at first, because I feared if I opened up the gate to my feelings, I would drown in a flood of emotions and dissolve into nothing. And for a time, I did. By dissolving the "shoulds", the walls around my heart began to drop. The old thoughts and beliefs shifted about who I *thought* I was, and what I "should" do. I was able to tap into the REAL me.

REAL
Realized Energies Aligned with Love

What I learned is that by diving into Self-Awareness, I created Self-Care. I learned how to connect to my Self, to love my Self, and to honor and respect my Self. I learned what I wanted, what I liked, and what worked for me.

Three steps became my saving grace in creating my Self-Care:

- **Meditate.** Take pure quiet time each day to connect with your Self, your Spirit Guides, and with the Universe (God, Higher Power, however you relate to this). Be in the "wordlessness" and listen.

- **Journal.** Do this first thing every morning as it's the time when your subconscious is closest to the surface and will reveal messages. Let your pen write, so you can discover what you're *truly* thinking and feeling. This helps you see what's really running you, so you can address it. Plus, it's an opportunity to download new inspirations and ideas.

- **Energetic healing.** Allow your Self to go within and release the energies of the past (including past lives). This creates a space and the freedom to move forward without the baggage that keeps you stuck. Energy healing practitioners and coaches can help you see things that you don't. Once you complete an old energetic cycle, you are done with it for good. There is no longer a need to re-create the old experiences or results.

If you're not aware of what's truly going on within you, then your physical body will break down, causing exhaustion, pain, illness, disorders, and disease, to name a few. Your emotional and mental bodies will not have the well-being, love, joy, harmony, or peace that you desire. This causes even more stress, struggle, and suffering, which leads to more unhappiness, lack of fulfillment, and overall dissatisfaction in all facets of your life.

The good news is by embarking on a Self-Awareness journey, this all can change. As I continued my in-depth exploration, healing work, and Self-Care, I discovered my True purpose and passion. While the 20 years of my corporate life was invaluable, it's not what I'm ultimately here to do.

In 2001, I was preparing to lead a group to swim with the dolphins in Bimini. Two days before leaving, I downloaded a set of symbols. I had no idea what they were, or what they did. I was given 'instructions' as to what to do with them once I was in Bimini.

Once I returned from Bimini, I was guided that I would use these symbols to help my Self first in my own healing and spiritual journey, then I would teach others how to use them. When I was guided in the early days of my search for who I was and what I was here to do, I usually went 'kicking and screaming' all the way. I usually acquiesced, since I knew that what I did in the past didn't work, so I was willing to try anything different.

However, I wasn't always the 'willing' participant. Many times I argued with the Divine and my Soul as to what I was being asked to do. My personality/egoic Self (P/E Self) liked things just the way they were, even though I was unhappy and unfulfilled. My P/E Self liked the 'familiar', even if it was uncomfortable and no longer served me.

My P/E Self liked to be in control and wanted to know who, what, when, how, and why, and this guidance thing was an unknown. My P/E Self wanted to avoid the unknown. This usually meant not listening to my intuition or guidance, playing it safe, and definitely not rocking the boat (especially with family and friends).

Well, my Soul was done with that! It reached out to my P/E Self and asked to co-create a new life and a new way of 'BE'-ing together. Over time, I learned how to trust my intuition, my Soul, and the guidance shared with me. I learned to trust *me* and *the Creator* within *me*.

Part of that journey was to discover my True purpose, which was to develop The Diamond Co-Creative System™ (the System) and share it with others. My mission is to help steward individuals to connect on a Soul level and with their Greater Soul's Purpose, Passion, and Plan, so they can prosper and thrive.

The symbols that came in at the time of my Bimini trip, were actually the Energy Codes (the Codes) which are components of the System. At the time when the Codes arrived, I felt totally shutdown, lacked clarity, and was uncertain of who I was and what I even wanted. I was first drawn to work with Code called *Connection*. It's truly where we all are called to begin our journey. The System helped me connect with both my Self and with the Universe (the Divine).

During my journey, I became more connected to my Soul's Essence, my Spirit Guides, and my purpose. I came to understand how the System helps you become more aware of your reason for being here, and the gifts you have to offer. It contains the Codes to help you create freedom within you, and for your life.

The System originates from Sacred Geometry (and so do you!). Each Code and Template (such as the Universal Manifestation Template are different groupings of Codes) are comprised of Sacred Geometric technology, Universal light language, and sound vibrations. They operate within the construct of Divine Love, Universal Laws, and spiritual principles, AND science and physics. The Codes have their own unique Sacred Geometric symbols, which provide different qualities, vibrational frequencies, and purposes.

The System accelerates your journey to reach a deeper level of exploration, discovery, connection, feeling, and knowing. It assists you to Energize, Elevate and Evolve by ...

- **Transforming** any energies out of alignment with Love

- **Aligning** with your upgraded '5D' Divine Blueprint, Purpose & Plan

- **Manifesting** your Highest Order & fullest Diamond Potential to thrive & prosper

- **Expanding** into your MORE & emBODYing your SOUL's Essence

It does not compete with other modalities, or your spiritual practices—it only enhances them. Unlike other modalities that typically only address the symptoms, the System goes to the *root* of the problem. It helps you discover the *Core Origination Point* of an issue, pattern, imprint, encoding, conditioning, programming, etc., so the energetic cycle can be completed once and for all.

The System goes beyond the healing process, so you can create NEW manifestations with NEW energetics, which are now vibrationally congruent with your Soul's Essence, Highest Order, and fullest Diamond Potential. The Diamond ... *your* Divine Brilliance.

It provides the ability to evolve into your MORE. By utilizing the System, you have the freedom to co-create with the Divine and live in the Fifth Dimension ('5D') of love, joy, passion, prosperity, and abundance.

Here's one tool from the System that guided me along the way ... the Universal Manifestation Template (the Template).

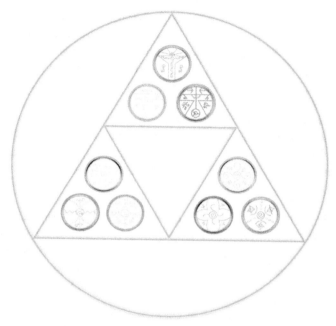

You can use this Template to heal, transform, create, manifest, and expand in any aspect of your life, relationships, health, finances, spirituality, career or business. Write your intention within the Template. Now, you've asked the Universe to advocate for and conspire with you. The Universe (the Divine and all your etheric helpers such as Spirit Guides and Angels) will help sort out and orchestrate what is your MORE.

Sometimes it's different than what you envisioned, but always (and I mean always) it's in Divine Truth and your Highest Order. As I sorted out who am I and what I wanted to do with the rest of my life, I placed a logo for a new business in the center of the Template. Within six weeks, everything about it fell away. There was no energy supporting it. It was a clear sign that this was *not* what I was to do. So, I refocused and created my current business ... it was a true blessing and saved me from a lot of frustration and heart ache trying to do something that wasn't in my best interest.

Here's another example of the Template revealing Divine Truth in relationships. I was on vacation for my birthday with someone I was dating. As I do each year, I was writing my birthday year vision. It included the kind of relationship I wanted with a Beloved. I was not 'attached' that it would be him, but of course, I hoped. I placed my vision in the Template.

Two hours later, he told me he didn't love me. Clearly not what I expected! But I had worked with the Template long enough to trust the process, so I easily let him go. I was relieved that I didn't waste one more minute on that relationship. Years later the love of my life from years before reemerged and we got married.

There are also times the Universe gives you MORE than you can imagine. Recently, my husband and I had to move. It was unexpected, and we didn't know how we were going to afford the move, or find a nice place in a very limited rental market. We wrote out our 'wish list' and placed it in the Template.

We had to only visit six places and it happened very quickly and easily. Our home is far beyond what we asked for ... perched on a hill overlooking the San Francisco Bay and Golden Gate Bridge. For two months, I had to pinch my Self to realize this is where we live and not simply on vacation, because of how breathtaking it is. We were actually given a whole new lifestyle, so the Universe gave us our MORE!

I've used the Template in my business, especially around the type of clients I want to work with, desired revenue, and to fill events. I held a retreat where I hoped for 22 or more participants and ended up with 44! I had to keep setting new intentions as I understood the Universe wanted MORE people to attend, and to give me MORE.

It's so much fun seeing the bigger picture that the Universe has for you! I invite you to add the Template to your Self-Awareness = Self-Care practice, so you can create your Freedom Code and manifest your MORE!

My wish for you is to manifest your True desires in all aspects of your life, health and well-being, and career or business, so you can prosper and thrive beyond your imagination! **You can download your Manifestation Template and ways to 'play' with it for FREE at: https:// CoCreateYourSuccess.com/ManifestYourMORE**

Amanda Slade

Amanda Slade is the founder of Co-Create Your Success and the developer of The Diamond Co-Creative System™ designed to offer SOUL-Aligned Possibilities and SOUL-utions to Energize, Elevate, and Evolve your health, well-being, relationships, and career or business. As a Transitions Leader and Evolution Catalyst, she helps steward individuals and groups to step MORE into their Brilliance, so they can be of service and contribution to the success of others and the planet.

For over two decades, Amanda has facilitated energetic healing, transformation, and spiritual growth with thousands of clients internationally, so they prosper and thrive. She co-creates with a team of Guides, Ascended Masters, and a Unity Council of 12 to help individuals with their evolutionary process. She has traveled as far away as Australia to teach The Diamond Co-Creative System™ which accelerates Transformation, Alignment, Manifestation, and Expansion.

Amanda has been featured on The Shift Network and multiple tele-summits, radio shows, and podcasts. She is a frequent presenter at business and spiritual events. She is a contributing author to the books, *Healing Body Mind and Soul: Empowered Self-Care* and *You Will Overcome*, along with articles featured in various publications.

She has 20 years of corporate experience and achieved success as a VP of Sales and Marketing for a New York publishing firm. Amanda's executive expertise brings both grounding and practical application to the "woo" factor, so her clients co-create success in all aspects of their lives.

Email: **Amanda@CoCreateYourSuccess.com**
Tel: 415-426-9764
Website: **https://cocreateyoursuccess.com**
Facebook: **https://www.facebook.com/ cocreateyoursuccesswithamandaslade/**
LinkedIn: **www.linkedin.com/in/amandaslade**
Twitter: @YourDiamondLife
You Tube: Amanda Slade

CLOSING THOUGHTS

We hope you have been inspired by the intricately beautiful and multi-faceted richness of this manual for empowered self-care and soulful living. It is our hope that you will be inspired to embrace your own self-healing journey back to your soul's divine essence in order to live your best life ever in a beautiful and peaceful world.

If this book has inspired you, we want to hear from you! Please don't keep it to yourself. Give it as a gift to someone you love or share a few kind words on our social media pages to help us raise awareness of our book and heal the planet.

We would love to know more about you and what fresh perspective you are taking in your own self-care practice as a result of reading and experiencing this book. What amazing results will you create in your world as a result of practicing radical self-care techniques?

Please be sure to join in on the conversation at one of our upcoming virtual book club discussions, one of our motivational summits, or just keep up on our weekly *Healing Body Mind and Soul* podcast, which you can subscribe to here: **https://bodymindsoul.tv/subscribe**

Connect with us on Facebook in our public group, Healing Body Mind and Soul Community:

https://www.facebook.com/groups/hbmsnetworkcommunity

Dear Heart-Centered Reader,

Thank you for reading our beautiful Empowered Self-Care anthology. I hope it has empowered, inspired, and helped you focus on what is really important . . . You!

I wanted to share a little bit more about *The Healing Body Mind and Soul* podcast and the BodyMindSoul.TV & Media Network Group. We are committed to supporting the voice of healing on the planet. I hope this book has not only supported you as a leader to take a fresh perspective on your own self-care, but also inspired you to plot a course for bringing your own voice forward onto the global stage.

If you want to reach more people and be part of healing and inspiring others with your story, your gifts, and the work that you bring to the world, then I want to share some opportunities for you to consider.

Each year, we compile and produce an anthology to support healing on the planet as well as spotlight and support the co-authors as they bring their work forward. We also produce a live streaming online TV show, facilitate speaker conferences, and conduct feature podcast interviews. In other words, we help experts like yourself step powerfully into the spotlight from a position of influence so they can make a global difference.

We provide group programs and strategies to help you get your voice heard and get your healing work seen by our audience and affiliated networks. We would love to support you in reaching more people to raise awareness of your work and also to raise the consciousness of the planet. Please take a moment to learn a bit more about our efforts at the sites listed below, and then reach out to us for a conversation. **We would love to help you show up, speak up, and stand out. Isn't it time the world heard your story?**

If you would like to connect with me personally to explore some of our opportunities in upcoming book projects, speaker success training, podcast production training, podcast interview opportunities, feature speaker spots in our summits, or one-on-one coaching, then please reach out to schedule a time to speak with me directly.

Please subscribe to our network: https://bodymindsoul.tv/subscribe

Check out upcoming co-author book publishing programs:

https://bodymindsoul.tv/book-publishing-program

Or learn more about my work: **www.AeriolAscher.com**

Email: AskAeriol@AeriolAscher.com

May you always choose to be seen, heard, and leave a legacy of love.

Happy Healing!

Warmly,

Aeriol Ascher

BEST SELLING ANTHOLOGIES FEATURING CHAPTERS BY AERIOL ASCHER

The Animal Legacies compiled by Rebecca Hall Gruyter

Experts and Influencers: The Leadership Edition compiled by Rebecca Hall Gruyter

Experts and Influencers: The Women's Empowerment Edition compiled by Rebecca Hall Gruyter

Experts and Influencers: Move Forward with Purpose Edition compiled by Rebecca Hall Gruyter (coming July 2021)

ANTHOLOGIES COMPILED BY AERIOL ASCHER

Empowered Self-Care: Healing, Body, Mind, and Soul for a Better World

Awakened Living: Stories of Self-Love, Healing, and Transformation (working title due out February 2022)

REVIEWS

"*Empowered Self-Care Healing, Body, Mind, and Soul for a Better World* is an amazing work of health, healing, and inspiration. The chapters are filled with something for everyone, inspiration, great tips, and strategies. You can open the book to any chapter, any page, and be inspired!"
—Diana Concoff Morgan
Whole Heart Marketing
www.wholeheartmarketing.com/

"Do you want to feel inspired? Do you want to be able to achieve the very best version of your true self? In this book, *Empowered Self-Care: Healing Body, Mind, and Soul for a Better World*, Aeriol Ascher and her co-authors take us on their personal journeys of growth and fulfillment. Together, they weave important messages, including practicing intentional choice and allowing the absolute best to happen to each of us. The co-authors share their individualized paths and teach us about the importance of relationships—not only with others, but most importantly with ourselves. The threads of self-awareness, self-care, and self-love are woven together in a beautiful tapestry of support that the readers will want to read and re-read. Not only will readers be inspired to do this for their daily lives, but also to gain continual inspiration for setting and achieving life-long goals."
—Wendy K. Benson, MBA, OTR/L and Elizabeth A. Myers, RN
2x2 Health: Private Health Concierge
http://www.2x2health.com/

"Aeriol Ascher has brought to the reader an amazing group of holistic healing practitioners, spiritual teachers, and transformational coaches who offer insights, tools, practices, and treatment plans to serve readers in their own daily self-care practice. Each story helps to unlock that inner-voice or intuition that allows us to become more comfortable in our physical bodies, heal past traumas, cure disease, clear anxiety, discover soul life, manage disappointment, and uplift life as we come to remember our true home lies within the heart. As holistic spiritual-ly-minded people know, each of us are continually moving from negative thoughts or experiences to find higher realms of love and happiness. In a duality of spiritual and physical life, we can find the ability to be calm, patient, and accepting of all challenges leading to a balanced lifestyle. The authors included in this anthology of holistic healers offer ways to achieve awareness, increase consciousness, and offer a means to live with authentic purpose, health, and joy. What could be better than to know how to become your best self?"

—Sheryl Glick
RMT Energy Practioner
www.sherylglick.com

"*Empowered Self-Care* could not come at a better time. Entering 2021 after a pandemic year, there are still so many uncertainties ahead of all mankind. This book will inspire others to look deep into their souls and start to change from the inside out. No longer will you worry about the images you once placed on yourself. You will release your old stories and began to create new ones. Each author touches on healing techniques that will add a spark and ignite a burning desire deep within your core, to make this year all about loving you, for you!"

—Karen Wright:
Author, Speaker, Healer, Lover of NOW
www.shinenowornever.com

"This anthology on empowered self-care compiled by Aeriol Ascher pulls together the life experiences and professional expertise of 25 healers in diversified fields to share their healing journeys. I love the panoptic aerial views and the complete body-mind-spirit coverage. What touched me most are the heartfelt and uplifting stories of healing from trauma that many co-authors share with the readers. Self-care starts from self-worth. There is no higher self-worth than recognizing the divinity within us. This book is a must-read for anyone who wants to heal holistically in order to live a vibrant life of well-being, love, and joy."
—**Sam Yau**
Poet
www.samyaupoetry.com

"A thought-provoking look at the concept of self-care and its effect on the body, mind, and soul. This book is for anyone who is looking for guidance on how to begin the path of self-care and healing themselves from within."
—**Maureen Ryan Blake**
Founder of The Power of the Tribe
https://thepowerofthetribe.com

"Self-care is an essential skill, especially in relationships! Relationships are everywhere with ourselves, our partner, our families, our friendships, our communities, and at work. The root of being successful in all of these is being integrated with ourselves. We must learn how to be truly authentic with our needs and desires and learn how to communicate that to the people in our lives. Every day I work with people suffering from relationship challenges and want to create better relationships. They spend an enormous amount of energy managing their feelings and navigating these challenges. This keeps them from radiating their light to the world. Aeriol Ascher has pulled together a powerful collection of specialists in self-care who share their stories, wisdom, and hope to guide you in how to care for yourself in our complex world. This self-care book is a must have to support you in creating the life your heart desires!"
—**Kimi Avary**
Relationship Navigation Specialist
Https://KimiAvary.com

"Empowerment is required in the pursuit of claiming the self-power that was initially been given away willingly or unwillingly. It is my hope that by reading this collection of work by inspiring authors, one would not only find their way back to their innate power, but pass on that lived experience of owning their power to the next generation by encouraging and cultivating the power of each soul."

—Dr. Kasthuri Henry, PhD

"I truly enjoyed reading these chapters. The book is packed with masterfully designed chapters from doctors and health practitioners that include daily powerful health techniques, meditation practices, and other resources to elevate your energy and your health. Great read on self-care, self-respect, and self-empowerment!"

—Elle Ballard
Founder of Women of the World Network
www.elleballard.com

"Discovering a fabulous book brings me joy. *Empowered Self-Care: Healing, Body, Mind and Soul for a Better World* fits the fabulous book category. Each co-author provides a window into their personal struggles, triumphs, and transformation. I was inspired, moved to tears, moved to laughter, and uplifted by the practical tools that were offered. I know this book will not sit idle on my bookshelf; it will be on my coffee table, ready to be opened to the random chapter that will inspire me that day."

—Karen Renee Halseth
Leaders Beyond Limits: Illuminate Your Innate Brilliance
karenrenee@leadersbeyondlimits.com

Made in the USA
Monee, IL
28 March 2021